Lost & Found

A Memoir

David L. Johnson Jr.

Lost & Found

ISBN 978-0-615-33498-1

Published by Davis Boy Publishing

Cover typeface: Scrum Bucket

Dedicated to

My two children Big Boy and Dajah

Love you both now and forever

- Daddy

Acknowledgments

To my children, you have shown a tremendous amount of support, love and loyalty to me. You have been my breath of fresh air for the past 6 years and I hope you continue to help me breathe for the rest of our lives. There are no others like you. Big Boy & Dajah.

-With all of my love, Daddy

A special thanks to Jenny Frost who introduced me to the idea of writing a memoir. I can't thank you enough for the support & direction that you and your best editor, Heather Jackson provided me with.

Lost & Found

Introduction

My memoir is not formatted in your typical autobiographical kind of way. I am allowing you to enter my thoughts as they come to me. My past & present is delivered to you as if I was being interviewed and asked questions by Barbara Walters or Larry King. Better yet—sitting on the stage with Oprah.

Be my doctor and allow yourself to become a therapist. Listen to my pain. Listen to my heart speak as if I was your first and last client that you will ever have. Read my memoir Lost & Found for what it is opposed to what you would want it to be.

David

Lost & Found

Note

Please excuse my approach when I am speaking about the different topics that concern me. Understand when I say you, they, White people or Black people that I do not mean it directly to the reader. My thoughts are concluded by my experiences.

Please do not take any offense.

Lost & Found

The story begins...

June 15th 1983, the day a baby boy was born lost to a pack of wild wolves.

My name is David Lee Johnson. I was not really born to a pack of wild wolves but I can honestly say that I was born to a pack of wild people. I'm the son of Donnie Johnson (Pete) and Irene Anderson. Brother of Derk, Darnell, Brian (Spunky). Here is where my story begins. Well… at least from where I can remember it beginning.

At three years old I remember our family living in an old Victorian house on 2nd St. in a small town named Woodland. Woodland is a very historical city. It was somewhat of a country looking city back when we lived there. A lot of factories were located there for some reason. This old city was known for its random hunting. I believe that the spirit/ghost were old souls that has not yet crossed over. If you ask me, it is a very eerie place that possessed a lot of character within. In the house we lived in, I can assure you that it was hunted. I remember seeing a Pink ghost repeatedly going through a wall in my parent's room. Some of you are most likely assuming that this is not true. I called you people "nonbelievers." At the time of my sighting I was only three years old. That confirms to me that I really saw what I thought I saw. The super natural seems to always make their present known to young children of the world, probably because of their open mind, heart and soul. Have you ever watched a baby look up at nothing and then instantly begin to crack laughing? Well, let me be the first to tell you, it is not you that they are seeing. They are seeing something that we adults do not have the privilege to see anymore, do to our lack of faith. Angels, spirits, ghost… whatever you want to call them, are around us everyday all day.

Woodland is located right outside of California's capital city (Sacramento).

I remember my mom and dad would always go hang out in the "alley" right next to the Olive Plant with all of their family, friends and foes. I remember the Olive Plant being guarded by very angry vicious Pit bulls that would attempt to attach anything and anyone that came near the metals fence in which they protected. It was really scaring because whenever they would through their bodies against the gate with rage, the fence would bend. My parents would leave my brothers and I at home while they roam these cold, deadly, backstabbing streets. Although I never understood why anyone would even consider hanging out there, we sometimes had no other options. My brothers and I had to spend a lot of time there watching, observing and learning from these drug dealers, murderers and crack heads. This was our home whenever we were evicted from our residence. Just think...we moved over 24 times by the time I reached age thirteen. Despite the violence that often took place right in front of our eyes we managed to ignore the frigid cold that we had to endure. Every night someone in the alley would throw trash, broken branches or whatever could be found into an old steel bin and set fire to it. My brothers and I would stand around the fire, having a full blown conversation with our eyes because we were told to "shut the fuck up... and stay in a kids place." That was the best advice that we were ever given because most of the violent acts would occur when someone spoke out of term or spoke rudely to each other. Watching grown men and women scratch, stab and punch each others teeth out of their mouths was like watching the devils demons when they're at their best. Watching though the flames of a nob fire did not make it any less believable. It was hell on earth and there is no other way to put it. This is just the beginning…and it gets worse before it gets better.

We moved to Davis ca in the summer of 1989.

Let me tell you a little bit about Davis. The original name for this place is Davisville. That should explain it all for you but for the ones who do not understand…the racial demographics is 100:1 white people to black people. By the way, those are the current demographics. Back in '89, we were one of the only 4 black families living in the whole city or should I say town. The other three Black families moved from Oakland ca, Texas and Dunagan ca. The temperature here averages at 105 degrees during the day and at night the degrees barely dropped. Living in a two bedroom tiny apartment that smelled like boiling chicken, with a total of six people…made the temperature even more unbearable. We did not turn on the wall mount A.C because we did not have the money to pay for it. Instead, we soaked wet cloths in cold water and place them on our fan. That worked for us temporarily. Waiting on the fan to rotate back and forth to all of our directions, drove us crazy. That alone, caused fist fights between us brothers. Our mom would make us stay outside in the blistering heat, all day. My brothers and I would be so hungry. We begin to watch the bird's activity. What they would eat, we would eat. The fruit trees quickly became our main source of food. When we became thirsty, we had to drink from a water fountain at the nearby park. The water tasted horrible and had the smell of a melting penny. The water was also very hot. The fountain was made of metal and it set directly in the sun. Therefore, it took 10 minutes, for the water to even begin to cool down. So, Instead of waiting, we would just drink the hot water. On occasion, we would arrive home a little later then what we expected. On those days, night fall would hit without one of us noticing. In our brains, we believed we were Ninjas. We always played in the dirt fields, attempting to run and jump over every trench, as if they were rivers. I remember the big clumps of dirt rock, smelled good to me, for some reason. My brothers would laugh because I would fall purposely in the dirt so I could catch a quick whiff. One night, while exploring new places, we came across a gathering. In the far distance, we could see fire burning on sticks. Smoke slowly rose into the sky and disappeared. People were dressed up in white sheet like clothing. White sheets covered their heads as well. At the age of six, I did not know what I was seeing and neither did my brothers, age's nine, ten and twelve. We were green to that kind of gathering and for some reason we knew to stay away. When we got home that night, we informed our parents of what we saw. In response, my dad said "stay away from those people." As if I we could not figure that much out. Our parents thought we were deaf, dumb and blind.

Being at home was very depressing. My mom and dad would argue, fuss and fight, every single day. The fighting would keep us up all through the night. The only time the arguing would stop, is while they were high on Crack rock. Even then, they would pretend to argue, so that everything would seem normal. I cannot believe that they would actually think that they could hide being extremely paranoid, very jumpy and sweaty.

Back then my mom was also a very bad alcoholic and still is. Her addiction to pills made the situation worse. Morphine, Percocet, Soma, Valium, Vicodin and many more, truly added pain to my little heart. When she would drink, the wolf would come out in her. After a few shots of E&J mixed with a few pills, the "wolf in heat" would come out of her.

The problem with that is…my dad was literally the big, bad, wolf. He is normally a very loving, kind, understanding person but once that button is pressed…may God be with you. My dad's knuckles were registered by the time he reached the age of seventeen. His hands are still registered in the system as deadly weapons, until this day.

Now, I want you to close your eyes and pretend to be me as a child for a while. You're a six year old child, having no choice but to stay awake, because of a party. By the way, it's your parents who are the ones are having the party! The music is so loud… all the walls in the house are vibrating. The smell of hard liquor, cigarette smoke and cheap perfume slowly fill the air in your bedroom. A different drunk person every ten minutes reopening your bedroom door and says "Oh shit, this ain't the bathroom." Right when you start to begin to adjust to the loud noises… you hear a scream, gunshot or someone say "I'm fenna kill this mutha fucka!" That's not where it ends! All the commotion is over your mom not using good judgment and being so intoxicated that she can barely stand. Oh, and being a complete slut. Come on now…follow me, the story is not over yet. My brother's and I got out of bed to see what was going on. As we peeked down the hallway into the living room, we begin to lose our balance and stumble over each other. As we watch a man lie lifeless and not moving, on our living room floor, my heart beat begin to race. Then you see someone throw a bucket of water on his face and said "wake your bitch ass up!" and that exactly what he did. Why was this man laying there unconscious? Well…that big bad wolf that I told you about, button was pressed one too many times. After everything died down, my brothers and I would get back into to bed. I remember saying to myself "I'm never going to get a girlfriend that act like her." And I stuck to my word.

These kinds of things happened in front of us on a regular basis. Can you picture it? I hope not, because these memories haunt me every single day of my life.

I remember my first day of first grade very well but I remember the day before even better. This year, I did not have any new clothes. I received handy downs from my older brothers, like every other poor kid in America. This story is not about what I had to wear, it is about what my parents did to keep our cloths clean. As you already figured out, we were a very poor family. We did not have enough money to take our clothes across the street to the Laundry room. Instead, my dad placed our clothes in an old white bucket, filled with hot water and poor in some lemon scented dish soap. To make sure that our clothes were actually being washed clean, he would also poor in a couple caps full of bleach. He would go get the toilet plunger out of the bathroom, rinse it off and begin plunging our clothes in the bucket. I must admit, that technique worked really well. The water in the bucket quickly darkened as he plunged. After 20 minutes of acting of a washer machine, he pulled our cloths out of the bucket and told us to help him ring them out. That part was fun because that was truly one of the only times I saw my dad really enjoy himself. When the process was done, our clothes smelled very clean. Our clothes were so clean sometimes, other kids would say, "you smell like soap." See, things like this confuse me. You try to keep our clothes clean but you forget about giving us baths. I cannot remember taking a single bath as a child. The only bath I remember taking was when my brothers and I would be dropped off at our grandma's house in Vallejo ca. That's where we would go when my mom finally got over the hump that my grandma wanted to take us from her. Hell, my mom should have willingly given us to her. When we were there, we were bathed, we went to church and we even had our own bed to sleep in. I love my Grandma and all she tried to do for us. Anyhow, the name of my elementary school was Valley Oak. We lived directly across the street from the school and I still arrived late to class. I blame that on my parents. That day was really embarrassing because all the kids stared at me like I was a mutant from another galaxy. Being the only black kid in my class caused heartache, but it has also caused me a lifetime of understanding. If I could rewind time, I would go through it all over again. My teacher name was Mrs. Campbell. She was very young for a teacher. She was white and from what I remembered she had honey brown/goldish hair. She would use a hair clip to put her hair up every day after we came in from lunch. Maybe because after lunch she would read to our class and she did not want her long hair to be in the way. Why do I remember this? I do not know. Anyhow, I loved it when she would read to the class because that was the only time anyone would read to me. In my eyes, she was reading the story directly to me. I often became intrigued by her facial expressions, movements and her passion of reading to us. The book was just something that she was holding in her hand. Sometimes she would catch me day dreaming and say, "Are you paying attention David J?" Then she would smile. I would just nod my head up and down, while I sat Indian style on the carpet. The room would always smell really good because Mrs. Campbell would always have the best smelling lotions. I could tell that she knew I came from a troubled background. Not because of my behavior nor by the way I dressed... but by looking into my eyes. My dad attended my first and only parent meeting conference that year. My dad and I sat down at her desk and I listened to her brag about me as if I were her first born son. Hearing that brought tears to my eyes because that was the first time that anyone had ever looked into my eyes and told me how great, smart and charming I am. That moment obviously stuck with me, because my fiance often calls me "cocky." I'm not cocky, I'm just confident. Now that I think back, I had a crush on my first grade teacher... but at the same time I wanted her to be my mom. Sounds crazy, I know.

That same year, in that same class, I met Joshua Adam Cooper. "What's up G?" is what he said to me while we were waiting in line to come in from recess. I looked back excited to finally see another black kid, but instead I was in for a shocking surprise. Josh is the whitest of all white kids. His hair was so blond, that it sometimes looked green. He would often wear a Green bay Packers pro hat, turned to the side or hiked up high on his head. At first I thought he was just being a smart ass and trying to mimic the way he thought black people spoke. With that in my brain, I just turned back around to face the front of the line. Seconds later he tapped me on my shoulder and said "My name is

Josh, what's your name?" I turned around and look at him for a few seconds and said "I'm David but my family calls me Lil'Dave." "Lil'Dave? That name is fresh." He said. Josh was some kid! He was my first friend. He was the first person that invited me to stay the night at his house. He was the first person to introduce me to country music. Garth Brooks "When the thunder Rolls." I still love that song. As Josh and I grew older, we grew apart. Although, the love that we had for each other never parted, we did…in terms of hanging out with each other. By the time we reached the eighth grade, Josh was in and out of Juvenile hall. Josh was adopted at the age of five and he had a lot of problems that no one could quite understand. His parents were great people and they loved him unconditionally. He was way ahead of his time. Josh died a few years after high school from heart failure. He was found dead on the bed next to a crying baby, at his girlfriend's house. I remember him telling me about his bad heart in the first grade. I recently took my family Jessica and our two kids David lll and Dajah to visit his grave. On Josh's tombstone sat a picture wedged into the grass for stability. The picture was of a little boy… who looked a lot like the Josh that I met in the first grade. I was hesitant to pick up the picture but something in the back of my mind told me to do it away. As I looked closely at the picture, it became evident to me that Josh had a son, that he never had a chance to introduce me to. On the back of the picture read, "Quincy's Kindergarten school picture." Quincy sure does look a lot like his father. They both have the same cow-lick on the front right side of their heads. Josh lives on through Quincy.

To the right of Josh's grave rest Jason Gregory Paz. Jason was my only other best friend, besides Josh. I met Jason in the seventh grade and we instantly connected. We played on the same basketball team. I introduced Josh to Jason and they both connected as well. From that day forth, we all three loved each other like brothers, until one day out of the blue…a tragedy occurred. Josh and I were left traumatized for the rest of our lives. I'm getting a head of myself. Let me finish telling you about my unusual life as a child. Hey, but don't worry, I will be sure to finish this story a little later.

Anyhow, Valley Oak elementary would let out from school every day at 3:05pm. I would watch all the kids being picked up by their parents, while my brothers and I would stand around & pretend to be waiting for our ride home. We sometimes waited until the last kid at our school is picked before we started our journey. Most of the time we would play basketball until the school grounds was completely empty. As the hours past, so did our teachers. "I'll see you guys tomorrow" they all yelled, waving their hands in the air from across the school. They all seemed to have the same routine every day. My teacher would leave first "Bye Mrs. Campbell" I would say loudly, then turn to my brothers and say "Dats my teacher" with a big smile on my face. Then Mr. Anderson would pass by. That was my Brother Brian's 4th grade teacher. I remember Mr. Anderson very well. He was the first and only Black teacher ever to work for the Davis School district, up until I graduated from high school. I also remember him because my mom would always try to flirt with him whenever she had a chance. Mr. Anderson was one of the few men that refuse to give in to mom's hourglass shape and sparkling white teeth. He reminds me of a dark skin President Obama. Mr. Milly would soon shortly walk by after Mr. Anderson. Mr.Milly was my brother Darnell's 5th grade teacher. Mr. Milly was and still is a sports fanatic. He's a white man that is built like a race horse. His voice is just as deep as James Earl Jones's. Come to think about it…it might be a little deeper. Seriously, I am not joking. Mr. Milly supported us in whatever we did. When he looked into our eyes and said something…we could tell that he meant it, with good intentions. He kept a close eye on all four of us. Marla would always leave last. Marla was my oldest brother Derk's 6th grade teacher. She would sit in her classroom listening to classical music and grading school papers for hours. She was an older white lady. She was somewhere in her early 60's then. She actually looked great for her age. She had long straight brownish gray hair that she never wore up. After the last teacher would pass us by, we figured it would be good for us to start our journey home, before it got too late. By the way, we moved at least three times since living across the street from the school. Back to the subject, by the time we make it home, our parents are gone. On the counter they would leave the same old note. "Darnell, you clean the kitchen! Spunky, you clean the bathroom and Lil'Dave you take out the trash....and I want the house spick & span when I get home." The way she closed her notes is what hurt me the most. All it would read is "Irene." Not an "I hope you boys had fun at school" or "I can't wait to see you guys when we get home." Nothing!! Just..."Irene" but for whatever reason I was happy with just that. I was not too worried about my mom and Dad because they always managed to call around 7:00pm or 8:00pm and check up on us. Every time they called, the same line comes out of their mouths "Lock the door and don't open it for ANYONE! You'll know when it's us because we knock like this KNOCK-KNOCK knock-Knock.............KNOCK-knock." For dinner we would always eat a syrup sandwich or a pack of Top Ramen noodles each. As the food settles in our hungry stomachs, my brothers and I would manage to settle down and get some sleep.

Life for us got very bad sometimes and we thought that we had it the worst. If it were not for those commercials that showed how the starving Ethiopian kids lived...we would not have been grateful for what we had. Don't get me wrong, my mom would cook some fantastic meals, but that was only on the 1st of the month when she got her welfare checks or food stamps. She would give us dollar after dollar, to go to the store to buy a 15 cent piece of candy. We would normally get a pack of Now and Laters or a box of Lemon Heads. The left over change would go straight to her. We would go back and forth to the store so much, the clerks caught on to her scam. After a while the clerk would just give us free candy, so that we could not exchange welfare money for real money. That is pretty crazy. I did not understand the whole situation until I was twenty some odd years old. My parents were really weird like that. I swear my parents were from some other world. Their actions did not add up sometimes. It seemed to me, that they reacted at the spur of the moment about everything. For instance, I was having a really bad tooth ache one day. I complained to my dad about how much it hurt. He did not know what to do about it. I could see it all over his face that it hurt him to see me in so much pain. He expressed to my Mom about the tremendous amount of pain I was feeling. She too, did not know what to do, since at the time we did not have any form of dental coverage. They decided that I should be taken to a veterinarian. My parents pleaded with the veterinarian to pull my bad tooth out. The Veterinarian repeatedly said, "This is not a dental office for humans. I cannot do this." My dad pleaded with him more and more until the veterinarian gave in. The veterinarian kneeled down on one knee and said nicely, "What would you like to do about your tooth?" Holding my mouth, with dried up tears on my face; I said with a soft voice, "I want you to pull it out." The only reason I said that was because I thought it was the right thing to say. My brothers and I were taught our whole lives, to agree with whatever our parents said. If we did not agree, we would get a spanking when we got home. Before this, I had never been to a dentist. I barely knew what a dentist was. Anyhow, as I climbed onto the veterinarians tall office chair, I started to become afraid. I did not want to say anything because being afraid was not an option in my family. The veterinarian asked me once more very nicely before he got out his pliers/vice grips, "Are you sure you want to do this?" In response I said, "Yeah." Only if he knew, that I did not know any better. I am far from upset with the veterinarian, for his actions. He truly just wanted to help. My parents threw the "feel sorry for us, we are poor and my child is in pain card" on him. Any compassionate human being would have done what he was about to do. He placed the pliers on my tooth and he begins to tug. I moaned in pain. He stopped tugging and asked, "Are you doing okay?" I uttered back in response "uh huh." My mouth was wide open, so I could not actually speak. The veterinarian, sat still for a moment in deep thought, then looked up at my father. I could see it in the veterinarian's face that he did not want to be the one to do this. My father quickly said "keep going, keep going, he's alright." As he began to tug a little harder, I began to moan a little louder. This time, my father stopped him and said, "Do you have anything you can give him for pain?" The Veterinarian said, "Sir this is a veterinarian hospital, we treat animals...the numbing product that we have is made specifically for animals. I will not give that to a child." "Okay, well can you try to pull it out faster or something?" The Veterinarian turned to his drawer and pulled out a pair of vice grips. After that, the rest was history. My tooth was placed in a small envelope and out the door we went with cotton pads pressed on my gums. When I got home to look at my tooth, half of it was rotten to the root. That really concerns me. How can a six year old have such a bad tooth? Having my tooth pulled out of my mouth, did not make it any easier for me to trust anyone. Better yet, it did not make it any easier for me to trust a dentist. I did not visit a dentist, until five years later. When I was done with my x-rays, the dentist looked at them and said to my mom, "Your son has over thirteen cavities and four root canals & that's just what the x-ray is showing." Just thinking about it, rips me apart.

August, 1990. A day I will never forget.

When my Father would drive me and my brothers somewhere, he would always say, "Lil' Dave, you have to sit in the middle because you're the youngest." My brothers and I would argue about who gets to sit next to the window. The window seat was special because you get a nice view on long rides. My Father would always say…."Whenever you're with your brothers, it's OK to sit in the middle, but never sit in the middle if you're riding with anyone else because that's for girls." That makes me laugh till this day. Too bad I couldn't manage to persuade my Father into allowing me to have the window seat on this late evening. Sitting in the middle gave me too good of a view.

As we drove down this dark, long street in a 1971, two-door brown Monte Carlo....death happened so fast. She ran out into the street. I did not know that a stupid Red Pogo ball could cause death. She was killed by a 1971 brown two-door Monte Carlo. To be exact, she was killed by our 1971 brown two door Monte Carlo. I watched the impact. I watched her die. I witnessed her lifeless body fly into the air. I was only 7 years old at the time. People say children can see the paranormal. I'm positive I saw an angel carefully catch her soul out of mid-flight, before her little body responded back to gravity.

I was too young to see such a bloody death. Even worst...she was too young to die. She had to be no more than 4 years old. I can't even imagine the pain that her Father was feeling as he held her in his arms. "My God!!" That is what I heard come from his mouth, whenever he was able to catch his breath. These memories haunt me every day. If only I could...help. If only I could rewind time....and stop her from dying young. That night and years after, I would catch my dad crying by himself every now and again. I never really asked him what he was crying about, because I already knew…most of the time.

On the days, I did not know or understand why my father was quite or sitting alone, I would ask him what's wrong. On occasion I would ask my father about his life and how he grew up. He would strive to ignore me but it never worked. He is too much of a loving person to leave someone questioning and wondering if he has the answer. Well, for a while he was. Passionately, he would talk about his old life of crime. From his kneecap to his hipbone, rest a scar. The scar was so deep…his bone was visible. He would proudly say, "I took the pain for two whole days before I went to the hospital…and that was only because it was bleeding too much." Reasoning for this awful, harrowing piercing? He was robbing someone's house. The window was the "quickest way out," I guess? The nonfiction Rambo like stories that he shared, captivated the minds of everyone. Even some impenetrable street kings took heave. Me myself and I…was far different from the rest. I did not care for the stories as much as I did for the underlying reason that caused the stories to become reality. I think my dad knew that. "When I seven years old, she tied my hands behind my back to a pole. For hours and sometimes days I stayed in that same spot. She put some little rocks on the floor, so when I got tired of standing the rocks would make my knees bleed. While my hands were tied behind my back, she would always beat me with a belt, shoe or whatever she could get her hands on. She would be really mad when she finally caught me because of all the other times I would run away from her. I would let her catch me because I did not want my brothers to deal with it. I would let her take it out on me, so she didn't take it out on them." "There! Is there anything else you wanna know?" he said to me. "I don't like to think about it" he said. At the time I was speechless but now I would like to say a few things.

No, there is nothing else I would like to know but there is something I would like to tell you. First and foremost, it takes a man to express your feelings. Thank you for taking the time to talk to me...now I understand. Also, I am sorry for asking you so many questions. Next time I will wait until you decide to tell me. My life compared to his, must seem like heaven to him.

My mom's life on the other hand was pretty much...picture perfect, from what my mom's side of the family tells me. Therefore, there should be no excuses for the way she raised us. My Grandma was a grandchild of a slave in Alabama.

Before the slave owners passed away, they signed their land over to my great great Grandpa. Before my great great grandpa past away, he divided all of the land up between his six children. One of those six children was my Grandma's father—my Great Grandfather. How much land did the family have all together? I do not know. My Grandma said her and her cousins would walk so far into the distance that the naked eye was not able to see them anymore. By the time they were out of sight, they would be at another family member's house. If you can envision that a total of six times, it should help you estimate how much land our family owned. Adding to that, the slave owner ran a corporation on the land. It was called the Rick's Head Quarters. My Grandma's last name is Ricks which originated from the slave owners. At the time, fruit, vegetables and every organic food that you can imagine were grown on that land. From that land, food was shipped off throughout Alabama. I bet you are wondering where I'm going with this huh? Right!?? Okay, to make a long story short. My Grandma was raised by and around hard working people, her whole life. She grew up rich with love, land and food. Back then, if you had that…as a Black person, you were elite. She obviously passed those morals down to her children because four out of five of her children graduated from UC Davis, including herself. I must add…my aunts and uncles are very successful people. My uncle Keith is a Professor at Boise State University. My uncle Yul is a very established classical musician in Denmark Europe. He did work with John Malkcovich on the movie "Dancers upstairs." He is close with pretty much every popular actor in Hollywood. He even went out to dinner with Bill Clinton. My aunt Lateasha was a Police Officer for the Napa Valley police department for several years and also ran for mayor of Vallejo Ca twice. My aunt Poshi was a Police officer as well. Back to my mom, she did not graduate high school. She had five different children by five different fathers. That includes my little sister, who died at birth. I hate to think about these things but hey…like they say "the truth shall set you free." You know what, while we are on the topic of my mom, I should just go right ahead and tell you all about her. I hope by me explaining to you what my mom is like will help you have a better understanding to why it's a miracle that I am alive and completely sane. I would rather not talk about it, because at this moment I do not want to cry. However, I would be more than happy to allow you to read the poem I wrote to her a while back. The poem is called Dear Irene.

Dear Irene

Throughout my whole life, I have loved you. Not for a split second has my love altered. You have taught me things that no other person on this earth could ever attempt to teach me, and for that I am forever grateful. With that being said, you have displayed a lack of love, understanding and judgment.

The majority of my childhood memories often cause me frustration and heartache. I always think of the past, before I lay down to sleep. Inside I cry like a baby but on the outside I am as solid as a rock, just like you taught us. On a regular basis, I wonder how you could have done things differently for the better. Sometimes, I feel all clogged up inside and it makes it hard for me to breath. At this point, I know your reading this letter saying to yourself "what the hell is this boy talking about?" That's one of the things that punctured me most. Now that I'm an adult with children of my own, I have realized what love is and supposed to be like.

I do not know if you understand what kind of impact, you and your decisions had on my life? There is a part of me that is broken and cannot be fixed. There are so many different things I try to forgive you for.

I was only 6 years old, when you looked into my eyes and said "I hate you." You have no idea how that felt and what it did to me. The sad part about it is…you probably forgot and never even thought about asking. When I was around 4 or 5 years old, I remember looking at you and wondering to myself "how come you don't allow me to call you mom?" "Mom" I said, with no reply. "Mom" I said, and still received the same silence. "Irene" I said, and in response to your name you said "What do you want boy?" If calling you mom caused you some type of pain...I am deeply sorry, but on this day I felt the need to at least try. Try to see what it feels like to call your mom....mom. Trying did not help. Trying, ended up breaking my little heart. "I could never be that way to my child! I would rather burn in hell for ever first.

For 22 long years, you made me and everyone else believe that Pete was my biological father, when in fact you knew he was not. Why and how could you do this to me? To add insult to injury, after I got a DNA test to confirm, you said "It isn't any of your business and that test is a lie." You kept a deep, dark secret, for all of these years. I hope you can see that there is something extremely wrong with that? What is wrong? I know nothing about your life before my birth. Something had to have caused you to be this way? I will not go into detail out of respect, but you had 5 kids by 5 different fathers! Why did you think that was okay? I know you will never tell me, but I just felt I should try.

I forgive you for never saying sorry. I forgive you for not

giving us all of you. I forgive you, for you.

I forgive you for everything you have done......but I will not

forget.

Me

By/ David Johnson

Yes, that poem hurts but hey...how much can you say to
someone that will deny every bad experience that you had
with them.

November 1993, by this time I'm ten years old.

Basketball had already been a big part of my life. My talent
level was far more impressive than any ten year old kid that
anyone had ever seen in Northern California. I was very
short, with the limbs of a grown man. My arms hung down
to my knee caps. My hands could palm a pro basketball and
wore a size 10 ½ shoe. I was jumping up and hanging on 10
foot rims at this age. Shortly after that, I was catching single
handed alley-hoops, slamming it down like I was doing it for
years. Wow, looking back on it...it sounds impossible.
Later in life, an angel came into my life and showed me that

nothing is impossible. As I was saying, I give all of my basketball achievements over to my brothers. Playing, watching and learning the game from the older kids made me five times more advanced than the kids my age. The homeless alcoholics that lived in the park (Chest Nut Park) were far more aware of my basketball gifts long before anyone else. They would come and shoot around with me sometimes. I learned a lot from them. I remember one of the homeless men saying to me, "I've been watching you play basketball every day at this park and you've proven that you can beat them all playing basketball, now I want to hear about you beating them all with a pencil." I did not understand what that meant back then but like us all…with age, comes wisdom. I'm 26 years old now and I know exactly what that meant. What the homeless man was trying to tell me was that…basketball should not be my first option. My education should always come first and with whatever time I had left over, should go to the game. He spoke like a true, articulate, professor from Harvard University or something. The ironic part is that I remember him telling me that he used to be a teacher. Sorry to fall off topic but these people unexpectedly shaped my life, which I now love.

People like Elliot Winslow, Tygery, Ray, Matt Ballin, Rahillio and Jose were some of the people that I looked up to on and off the court. The people who hung out at the park were my family away from my family…you know? Oh, & I remember this kid named Gary, who would play me one-on-one every single day. He would beat me all the time. As my body developed, losing to him changed quickly. The best part about it is that he would pat me on my back and say, "Man! You have gotten a lot better." Thanks Gary…I needed that more than you could ever know.

My brothers and I would play basketball so hard against each other; it would lead to fist fights, bad language and even the silent treatment for days. We took the game serious. In our eyes, there was no such thing as losing. If I would lose while playing basketball at the park, or even in an organized game, my brothers would criticize me and tell me how unworthy I am to the game. "You ain't no baller! You hella weak! You garbage Lil'Dave! Step ya game up boy! You ain't ready yet!" It is crazy because even when I dominated the game, I would still receive those harsh words. With all that being said, I knew all they were trying to do, is explain to me that being good is not good enough. Being the best does not mean you are the best. Being able to toy with the greatest, means you are ready.

Damn, those were some high standards to try to live up to. With practice, my brothers believed it could be done. I figured, the best way to live up to these standards, were to immolate what the standard setters did every day. Boy, was I in for a big surprise! I cannot even begin to describe the workouts they were doing; mind you, we were children at the time. We ran so many flights of stairs, my legs went numb. I felt like a ghost floating up the steps. My legs were completely dead. We did cliometrics, ball handling, shooting drills, slides and then played a game called 21. I am not done yet, that is what we did earlier in the day, at Hickey gym. Around 4:00pm, we would ride our bikes back across town to our neighborhood park, where the true basketball players played. That is when I wanted to play most, but they would not let me. They thought I would get hurt or something. I remember sitting on my ball with my back against the pole, admiring my big bothers. Although, my brothers and I have not spoken in years…I will never forget those days.

On some days, it would get up to 116 degrees. We would play basketball for so long on the black top that our feet would feel like they were on fire. All of the sudden stopping and going, sliding and jumping would cause a lot of heat and friction on our feet. It would get so hot that my brothers and I would rush to the grass and take our shoes off to cool our feet down. My brother Brian...he would never take his shoes off. Not because he did not want to, but because he was too embarrassed to do so. Let me explain. My brother is completely covered with third degree burns from the tip of his toes to the beginning of his calves. The scars on his feet look very similar to a person who may have been doused with lighter fluid and then set in flames for a long period of time. Although the story that our mom gave us to explain the reasoning for this severe burn, does not make any damn sense...just like every other word that comes out of her mouth. Her side of story consist of this...and I quote "when I was gone one night, my ex boyfriend Brian Sr. put him in hot water." She never answered any other questions or gave us any other answers besides that. When we would press the issue, she would say don't worry about it, it ain't none of y'all business." Damn she's a cold hearted person. God works in mysterious ways though. According to our mom, my brother's Darnell and Brian, share the same father

"genetically." There are a few glitches in that because...
Darnell has a very light skin complexion. He looks as if he
could be biracial. He is pretty much the same color as my
children, and my kids are half white. So, the possibility of
Brian Sr. being his Father is kind of out of the window
because Brian Sr. is as dark as the night itself. My mother
fits that description as well. I know black people are a race
of many skin colors and tones, but the probability of him
fathering a child of my brother Darnell's complexion...are
rare. It is very possible but not in this case. Another thing
that made no sense to any of us...is why would she name my
brother Brian, after their father, if Darnell is older.
Normally, people name their first born son after the father...
right? Goodness, here is another thing. They look absolutely
nothing alike. When I say nothing, I mean nothing! Not a
single hair on their head is similar, while my brother Brian
on the other hand, looked identical to Brian Sr. Again, there
are children in the world that look absolutely nothing like
their parents, so for a while we trusted our mom and gave
her the benefit of the doubt.

Until one day my brother Darnell was around 23 years old.
He did some research and found out where Brian Sr. lived.
He resided Indianapolis, Indiana. He owned a very nice
church that he preached at as well. This is how my brother

told me the story. "When I first saw him, I knew he was not my dad. He said he was not my dad. He said "Spunky" (Brian) was his son though." I asked Darnell, if he asked him if he knew what happened to our brother's feet. "I sure did and if he gave me some bullshit answer, I was going to punch him right in his fucking face" he said. So, "what was said," I asked him? Darnell answered, "He said, I didn't do that to his feet. Why would I do something like that to a child? When me and Irene was living together, I used to sell a lot of drugs and me and your mom would always argue because whenever I got home all of the drugs would be gone. Irene would use up all of the drugs and that took away from the money that we needed to pay the bills. Irene put your brother in hot bath water when she was high on drugs. She did not mean to, she was drugged up."

Oh my! I just remembered our mom actually had the audacity to conduct a spiritual cleansing, for my brother Brian's room, in an effort to remove the evil that she thought was in his room. In her eyes, the room possessed my brother because he is "mad all the time, he never talks to anyone and he stays in his room all the time." At the time, it did seem that way. Actually, it was that way but not because he was possessed! The reasoning behind his self isolation was because a hurt, confused, mistreated, lied to, abandoned and undernourished fifteen year old boy did not know how to react to such heartache.

Damn, this is hard for me to talk about. Well, anyways, that is the reason my brother never took his shoes off to cool his feet down in the grass. I guess we all have to play the cards that we were dealt. The hard part about playing the game of cards is playing with loved ones. One of the most difficult parts to stomach is realizing that the people you love most, could care less if you were dealt a bad hand. What takes even more strength is being able to acknowledge who the confused people are, pray for them, forgive them for what they have done and move on. I myself know that I have not religiously followed that regimen. Sometimes, there should no excuse to be made. All God wants to feel…is that you are sorry. Guess what? All people want, is to know that you are sorry. Think about that!

I wrote a poem with my brother in mind, and I would like to share it with you all. Hopefully, some day he will come across this poem and know it was written for him.

Life's Changes

Your lost like a baby duckling in search of its mother. Where life may take you…you do not know and neither does anyone else. You can strive in the direction that you would like to go, but it is only possible, if it is God's will. Often, you are afraid of being free like the wind, although you dream to be one day. Terrified of where you may end up next, you clutch endearingly on to your security blanket. With the limited amount of strength you have left, life begins to take advantage of your weakness and pierce you, invariably like a thorn in the wild. Little does the atheist know…your life, bad dream, trials and or tribulations are not presented to you because of God's absentmindedness? More because of the strength God has chosen to provide you with. Hopefully you understand what I am trying to say. My advice for us all…is keeping our heads up, literally.

By/ David Johnson

September 1st 1995, was my first day of Junior High School. My first day of 7th grade was not the best day for me. It was actually very scary. It was a bigger school with more responsibilities and that scared me. My parents did not attend my registration the day before, so finding my way around campus was very difficult. After third period, I started to notice some familiar faces from my elementary school. By the end of the day, the whole school knew of me. Kids 7th through 9th grade would come up to me and say, "You're that kid that is really good at basketball, huh!?" My response would be, "something like that." After a while, it kind of got irritating that the only reason people knew who I was, was because of basketball. In my heart, I am more than just a good basketball player. I feel that way now and I felt the same way back then. I feel people should know who I am because of my loyalty. Love me…for having the heart to die for the ones I love. Care for me because of who I am, not because of what I can do. My rules in life are very simple. "Surround yourself by positive people, do positive things and positive things will happen." Reverend Malone.

My second day at school was one of my best days ever. For my 3rd period class, I had gym. I hated gym class! The gym was not really a gym. Our floors were not wood like every other gym in the world. Our floors were made of some rubber stuff that everyone carved bad words into. It smelled really bad and it did not have air condition. I did like the basketball hoops, although they had wood backboards

instead of the glass ones. Anyhow, I failed it every year.
Why did I not just do the extremely easy, pointless activities
that our teacher assigned us to do? I do not know. Probably
because my parents did not take school serious anyway. My
dad dropped out in the 7th grade and like I said before, my
mom did not finish high school. Or it could be because I
was a very stubborn kid. Who knows, but both of the
reasons are foolish. When the teacher made us all sit down
for roll call, I would just nod my head once, opposed to
raising my hand and saying, "here!" As the teachers went
down there list checking off names...I watched. I watched
each person they called. "Yea, I'm here" a boy calmly said
from behind me. I looked back because he was the first
person that I thought did not sound nerdy or giggly. When
I looked back, he looked at me as said "What's up?" "What's
up?" I replied. After I turned back around to face the
teacher, he slid up to the open spot right next to me and said
"Eh, do you know how to break dance?" "No, do you?" I
replied. "Yea, for a few years." he replied. He instantly busts
out and did a weird backspin. The backspin was not funny,
it was actually pretty cool. The part that cracked me up was
him being caught by the teacher. If only you could have seen
him doing his so called "Break dancing" move and be then
startled by the teachers yell, in the middle of spinning.

"Mrrrrrr PAZ!" the teacher said as he looks down at his name sheet to make sure he has the correct name. "Yeah, sorry" Jason replied as he stumbled out of his spin move looking like he saw a ghost. "Is that where you should be?" the teacher asked. "Sorry-- no, I'm getting back to my spot right now" Jason said while he slid back to his original spot. "Eh, I will talk to you after class" Jason whispered from behind me, which made me laugh more.

Yes, this is the Jason that I spoke of earlier. Like I said before, Jason, Josh and I were the best of friends. Jason spent five good years with us before he died in a fatal car crash at the beginning of our junior year in high school. When we entered high school, Jason found more friends that he felt he should share his time with. I was not too fond of his new friends but I understood because Jason was a people pleaser. He hated to see people go without having what they needed. I won Best smile and best dressed in the 9th grade. Why do you think I won "best dressed?" I'll tell you. Pretty much, every pair of pants, shirts and shoes that I owned, was given to me by him. Jason never once made me feel any less than a normal person for wearing his clothes. He never once asked for his clothes back. Honestly, I think he completely forgot about them. That's the kind of friend Jason was.

Clothes, money, popularity…all that meant nothing to him. Anyhow, a week prior to Jason's passing, I saw him one day while I was walking down the street. He pulled over beside me in his beautiful plum red 1998 Honda Prelude, yelling out of the window "Lil Dave! Eh Lil Dave!" Jason was the only person who called me Lil'Dave besides my family members. That was always Jason's ways of telling me that we were still best friends even though we did not hang out much anymore. As I rested my elbows inside of his passenger door window, we made it clear to each other that we needed to get together and hangout more, like old times. Before he drove off, I said…"I'm gonna get at you." In proper English, that means that I will be in contact with you soon. About a week later, Jason died in a car crash at around 5:00am. While his new friends that were in the car with him that early morning, walked away without a single scratch.

Jason was split down the middle by a phone pole. He flew 70 feet out of the car. His last words were, "Tell my mom I love her."

This is the part that I cannot let go of. Jason died 5 hours before I called to see if he wanted to hang out, like we talked about a week prior. If I would have not procrastinated on calling him…I know he would still be alive. That is how I feel some nights.

Three years after Jason's death I went to visit his parents with my week old son and Jessica, who is the Mother of my two children. When Jason's mother saw us, she had a shocked, happy and confused look on her face. I do not know if it was a surprise to see I had a child, or if she was shocked by how much Jessica and Jason resembled each other. They both had curly thick dark brown hair, olive skin complexion and exotic big green eyes. Either way, she cried and hugged us.

Although, Jason and Josh's death traumatized me, death was nothing new to me. Since early childhood, I've watched close people come and go. I was taught to block out my feelings, when it came to that. If heaven could receive postal mail, my letter to them would say this...

Dear Jason & Josh,

I can remember our days together so vividly. Your approach to life, has made me a stronger man for today & tomorrow. Although you are not here in human form to watch me cry, smile, and reminisce about our past times....I am certain that you guys and the man upstairs will look down on me. From the heavens my friend, you see the future, but from earth...all I can see is the past. They say "try to forget about the past because it distracts from the now." I say "easier said than done." I think of your fatherless child. I think of your companionless wife. "My Heavenly father...my heart hurts." Lord knows my heart goes out to your families. I have so many unanswered questions. "Lord, how can I be of use"? Memories of you both and I as adolescents are beginning to rekindle in my mind. Memories of us in deep conversation, continuously repeats. Memories of us laughing together, joking and being a family are now becoming clear. I must understand that you guys are gone to a better place. I cannot bring you back, but I sure can keep your memories alive until the next time we meet and embrace. I will continue to live life righteously...so when our day comes to reunite, I will have something to show for, during our time apart. I Love You Both!

Best friends forever,

Lil'Dave

I know my life is starting to become hard to believe, but every single word that I am saying is true. Sometimes, I can't believe it either. Listen closely because it gets deeper and deeper.

My biological father was shot in the chest. Pretty crazy…
huh? The bullet barely missed his heart. About one inch
higher… He managed to dodge the perpetrator, get into his
car and make it to the front of the UC Davis Medical
Center. Passing out from a loss of too much blood…the car
cruised into the emergency pole right in front of the
emergency room entrance. Damn….God is beautiful.

A good friend of the family, "Greg," was shot in the gut with
a sawed off shotgun. Standing no more than ten feet away…
this man survived. "Greg" was a really heavy set man with
the heart of a kid. I remember him like he was here
yesterday. He could drink with the best of them. When he
got drunk, he'd talk more shit than Gary Paton—the veteran
NBA player! He was a great guy. If you have not noticed, I
speak of Greg in a past tense sort of way. Yeah…Greg has
passed away. The gun shot couldn't kill him…he's just too
strong! The fat around his stomach is what stopped the buck
shots from penetrating. Greg had such a big beer belly. That
beer belly saved his life. That beer belly also killed him.
Years later, the liquor caught up to him, causing his kidneys
to fail. He taught me how to roll my stomach.

Then there was another family friend by the name of, "Les." I don't remember much about him besides....he would always wear a black baseball cap. Lesley would always blast his car music, open all of the doors and pretend to clean his car. I knew he was not cleaning his car. Although, everybody would always say, "Dat boy Lesley...always keep his car clean!" The truth is...Lesley wanted people to hear the crystal clear sound of his speakers pounding. That it was! It sounded like surround sound without the static. See...being from where he was from, life was hard. The only reason Lesley arrived in California was because he wanted a new beginning. He lived a whole life of crime in the past. The dirty south was his departure city. We all know once you leave...try to never come back. Les left, but he went back! Found dead...shot in the chest in front of his neighborhood liquor store.

1998 my freshmen year

This was the year basketball put me on the map. I was a 5'6 fourteen year old who threw down a flawless one handed slam dunk, against one of the best power house schools in California (Jesuit private school). Jesuit is an all boys school that recruits the best players in Northern California. I remember how cool their uniforms were. Red, white and gold were the colors that every school in the area feared. I did not blame some of my team mates for being afraid because Jesuit's basketball team looked like grown men. These kids already had full grown beards. Every single person on that team looked like a man child running around. They were big white kids, with muscles like Lebron James'. You have to believe me. Okay, maybe I am exaggerating a little, but not by much. Their basketball players played on the football team as well and that's why they were so damn big. Little did they know about a little black kid, who played on a little white team, that believed "the bigger they are, the harder they they'll fall." You have to keep in mind that I've been playing against older, bigger people my whole life...so playing against these guys was just another day in the park. Once that ball was thrown up, Jesuit knew that we were about business. Losing was not an option! Our coach Cam prepared us for that day, as if we were soldiers preparing for combat. I, myself, had the all the tools for combat. Cam came along and showed me how to utilize them in a respectful, controlled and smooth way. Cam is by far the best coach that I have ever had. I remember one day in the locker room before one of our basketball games, he sat us all down and gave a speech. The speech was not about basketball. The speech was about life and how far we have come, since the 40's and 50's. By the way, my basketball team called me D.J.

This is how his speech went. "You all know that D.J is the one and only black kid on our team. For pretty much all of you, being around D.J has allowed you a first time experience of being around a black person. I noticed how we all love each other on this team and how color has never been an issue but I would like to say a few things. 50 years ago, D.J. would have not been able to play on this basketball. The reason is because he is black. So before we go out and win this game, let's do it for D.J!!!! Let's do it for us as a family!!! Let's go kick some ass!!!!!"

That night like every other night, we blew that team out by 40 points. Our record that year was 40-2. The two losses we had, we redeemed ourselves and blew them out as well.

Soon after basketball for my school ended, Christmas would be coming right around the corner. I really enjoyed this particular year's Christmas because I was big enough and strong enough to do what I wanted to do. Spending Christmas with my family often made me think of the past. From age 6 and up, my brothers and I had to stand in the cold and sell mistletoes. My father would go riding around town on his bike, looking for trees that had mistletoe hanging from above. He would climb really high to cut down .batch after batch to wrap and prepare. He would place enough mistletoe to fill a sandwich bag and then seal it shut with a sticky bow. I remember looking at the different color bows and loving how they shined. Red, white, blue and gold bows kept hundreds of baggies filled with mistletoe sealed and shut tight. My dad worked really hard to gather and prepare the mistletoes for us to sell. With that being said, my brothers and I worked even harder to get rid of them. Our parents would drop us off in front of different grocery stores to sell them while they go back home or sit in the warm car to watch. During the winter time, it used to get really cold here in Davis, so we would wear layers of clothing. On our hands, we would have to wear socks because we did not have gloves. The socks worked pretty good keeping our hands warm, but the mittens that a stranger exiting the grocery store worked a lot better. She was an elderly white woman with blond hair and I remember her smelling really good (Warm Vanilla scent). She gave me a hug and said, "You are adorable. You must be freezing out here. I got you some things to keep you nice and warm. Here, put these on." She helped me put on the new mittens and earmuffs that she specifically just bought for me and handed me a $20 dollar bill. "Merry Christmas sweetie," she said as she turned and walked away. I stood there for a second, confused and wondering why a total stranger would care about someone like me. "Here, you forgot your mistletoes!" I tried to yell out but my body was too cold to get my words out. My body was shivering and it caused my teeth to chatter. Anyhow, she turned back in stride and said very softly, "You keep it," and then smiled. Damn, I love that lady for that.

We normally arrived home between the hours of 11:30pm or 1:00am. The time varied. It depended on how fast we sold our box filled with mistletoe. I told my parents about the nice lady that I met. I also told them about all the nice things she said. My parents instantly looked at me and saw a dollar sign. They instantly made us begin rehearsing what we would say to the customers leaving the store, "Excuse me sir/ma'am, would you like to buy mistletoe for $1.00? I'm trying to buy my Mom a VCR for Christmas." From that day forth, instead of giving me 100 mistletoes to sell, they doubled the amount. Doubling the amount meant that I had to stay in the cold twice as long. We normally started selling around 6:00pm, but after hearing about the kind lady I met, the time changed to 4:00pm. That gave us enough time to get home from school, eat something real quick and then hit the streets or should I say the stores. I am not a rocket scientist or a math whiz, but if I did not know any better, I would say that my brothers and I were being pimped. Okay, let's do the math together. There are 4 boys including myself. We all sold 200 mistletoes each, day in and day out for at least three weeks straight. They would sometimes go pick up my little cousin from Sacramento to help. He did not have to sell as many as we did. He got around 75 of them to sell. Okay, 200x4= 800. There is 7 days in each week, which means there is 21 days in three weeks. 800 mistletoe times 21 days equals 16,800 mistletoe. That means that my parents round up $16,800 in three weeks every time Christmas came around. I'm not even adding in the amount that my little cousin sold. Our Christmas gifts often consisted of a bottle of lotion, bar of soap, rubbing alcohol, deodorant and cotton swabs. I think to myself, "A) What the hell were my parents thinking getting a 7 year old deodorant, when I had not even reached puberty yet? B) What the hell did they do with all of that money?" By the way our "gifts" came from the dollar store, so they did not work too well. Our "gifts" were wrapped in newspaper. No Santa Clause or Rudolph the red nosed reindeer wrapping paper.

Now that we are talking about newspaper, I remember not having any toilet paper, so we had to use newspaper to wipe. To be completely honest, some of those days we actually did have toilet paper but our mom would save it for herself instead. I feel so bad for me as a child, but you better not. My life gets better.

After Christmas or after any other holiday passes, we would all go dumpster diving in the different dumpsters around Davis. We would hope that the wealthier people would get rid of their old belongings to make room for their new ones. I hated to dumpster dive because a lot of kids from my school would say, "Hey, I saw you and your dad in the big dumpster yesterday, what were you guys doing!" They did not mean it in a bad by what they said, but the question alone embarrassed me. They did not know what the hell we were doing. For all they knew, I was a helping my dad with his job. As a matter of fact, I remember kids at the school were standing in a circle talking about their parent's jobs. As I walked up, one kid said nicely, "Hey David, where does your dad work?" Before I could reply, another kid in the circle said nonchalantly, "His dad is trash man." Then they continued on with the conversation.

I believe by me being a star basketball player, it drew a lot of attention from the young ladies. Actually, being the only black kid at the whole school caused the girls to love me. I was exactly what their fathers did not want their daughters to bring home. A young black kid, with nappy hair who sagged his pants. I was not what their parents visualized their daughters kissing and hugging on. Seeing the excitement on their daughters faces whenever I was near, completely ate them up inside. I did not really care if it made them upset because I never chased the girls, they chased me. After the parents finally met me and got to know me, they would always invite me over for dinner. It's really cool because if I saw them today, they would invite me over even though their daughters are long gone and married with children. That is special and it means a lot to me. Having nice people like that to invite me over for dinner came in handy when the food was really low at my house. I lost a lot of friends and made a lot of enemies because of girls. In high school, I began to notice who my real friends were. My true friends were obviously Jason and Josh but I'm talking about my associates. High school in Davis starts in the 10th grade, although freshman sports use the high school facilities. My so called ninth grade associates completely stopped hanging out with me as soon as we graduated from Junior high. At first I did not understand why they abandoned me but after watching and observing, I quickly caught on. My high school population was really high. I was one of 7 black kids who attended my high school. That is not many considering that we had a total of 3,000 kids. Anyhow, I think my associates stopped hanging out with me because they did not think that all the other white kids would accept me because I was black. Little did they know, pretty much every kid at the school already knew of me. They wanted to know more. For a lot of these kids, I was the only black kid that they have every spoken with. They wanted to know everything about the black culture but I could not tell them much because my background has always been kind of...not good. Anyhow, after my associates noticed how the other kids took heave...they started speaking to me a lot more. I paid them no more attention.

Sorry to cut the story short about the girls I dated during school but you have to remember, I am in love with a very beautiful woman now. We have two children together and we plan to get married in the near future. Basically, I do not want to hear the whole, "Who is that? You never told me about that girl before."

Let me tell you all about the one of many times that my mom has brainwashed and imprisoned someone. This is how the story begins. My brother Derk used to like a girl named Annie. Annie had a friend named Christina that liked Derk. Christina was a very nice girl. She was very giving and understanding. The thing that hurt Christina the most, besides my mom…was her tendency to be easily influenced. She was overweight and mentally disabled. She was far from retarded but she caught on to things a little bit slower than the average person. I forget where Christina was from, but I know her parents lived in another state. That made her very vulnerable. Annie came to visit my brother Derk unexpectedly one day and brought Christina along. Bringing Christina along with her was the wrong thing to do. After that day, Christina would always come by looking for my brother. My brother always avoided her, until this one day. My parents convinced my brother Derk to use her for her money. They said, "Derk, don't be stupid, you can tell she likes you. Tell her to buy you something to show how much she cares. Just because she likes you doesn't mean you have to like her back fool." Derk is at the shallow end of the dream pool when it comes to standing his ground and being mind strong. Soon after that, my brother would come home with new clothes, DVD players and walkmans. All bought by Christina. After my mom realized that Christina was crazy over my brother, she starting using him to get to her. "Christina, you can stay the night. You go sleep in Derk's room." Knowing Christina, that was her fantasy. Christina would sleep in his room for weeks at a time and from as far as I know, they never had a sexual relationship. When my mom knew Christina was attached to my brother, she began to say disrespectful things to her. My mom would call her names like fat ass, retarded ass and many more names that I would rather not to say. After the name calling got old, she would make her clean the kitchen every day. Cleaning the kitchen quickly turned into cleaning the bathrooms, living room and my mom's room. Christina would do all of this because of her love for Derk. I felt so bad for her but what could I do? We were all under my mom's spell. Her loud screams, threats and stare would scare us in a very forceful way. The repetitiveness of all of that is what slowly trapped us all. Having something drilled into your head every single day, the exact same way can brainwash a person. If anyone in the house began to think on our own, she would use my dad to scare us, since he was really big. She has my dad brain washed until this day. You have to remember, my mom met and had sex with my dad Donnie the first night she met him. As a matter of fact, it was within a couple of hours before she was unbuttoning his pants. My dad told me that one night when he was drunk. My dad was 15 when he got together with my mom. My mom was 21. Those numbers alone explain the brain washing that she has put on my dad. Anyhow, back to the crazy story. Irene would make Christina sleep in an outdoor/indoor closet right next to her room. The scary part is that the door to her closet locked from the outside, not the inside. That means my mom had control over when Christina could come in and out. There was a door on the other side of the closet that led to our side yard, but they kept a bunch items barricaded up against the door so she could not get out. Months went by and Christina was at Irene's every command. Christina could not eat, use the bathroom or speak unless Irene said.

I could not take seeing this anymore, so one night when everyone was asleep…I crept around to the side of our house and moved everything to the side that was blocking her exit door shut. After I moved everything out of the way, I cracked the door and whispered to Christina, "The door is open, you can leave now." In response she said "Nooooo, I can't man. Irene will kill me." I left the door open and ran back around to my room. I had to watch a nice person being battered. I will never forgive myself for not calling the police. Being thirteen years old…I just did not know what to do. Christina soon picked up the heart to leave out of the side door for good, soon after that day.

As you can tell my life like is filled with crazy situations. My past is a very scary place to visit. The only reason I take it back there is because I believe in facing your fears even when you feel like you cannot beat them. After all, without fear there can be no courage.

My dad's grandparents were killed by his uncle. One day, he went crazy and shot them both with a shotgun. That is so sad. Anyhow, my mom would make fun of my dad because of this horrible tragedy. Whenever my mom would get upset with my day, she would say mean things to him like "You're a stupid, dumb motherfucker! You're crazy! Your whole family is crazy and that is why your uncle killed your grandparents." I felt really bad for my dad on those kinds of days because for some reason, he would not stick up for himself. Maybe my dad felt guilty for all the times he broke her jaw and that why he sits and takes her abuse. In my opinion, I would have liked to see him get up and leave.

Life sure does change us. Life can change us for the better and it can change us for the worst. Life always seems to get worst when things are already going bad. People come in and out of you're for a reason. Everything happens for a reason. I try to find the positive in a negative even though it is a difficult thing to do.

1998 This was the year I fell in love with sci-fi movies.

Sci-fi movies took me away from my everyday life. For hours at a time, it took me away from my past as well. This is when basketball was awesome for me. I was pulled up to play for the Varsity team even though I was only a sophomore. In Davis, being pulled up to play on a varsity team did not happen often. I played a few regular season games with the Varsity team and soon after that, I demoted myself back down to the Junior Varsity team. The varsity coach Villanova and I disagreed on a lot of different things when it came to basketball. Now that I am older, I realized that I had the problem. He knew a lot about the game of basketball and all I had to do is listen. That is one of my biggest regrets. Coach Villanova was great. I was just a kid who was anxious to play and he was a very patient coach. Learning to be patient was something I really needed back then but…I did not know it. Coach Villanova was preparing me for the Politics that comes along with the game of basketball. The thing I appreciate most about coach Villanova is that he would never let politics get the best of him. He would never allow the politics to do the coaching. The final decision was always made with his heart, on and off the court.

I cannot say the same thing about the Junior Varsity team head coach (Coach Martinez). The year I demoted myself down to play on his JV team, he did a great job coaching. My junior year in high school, coach Villanova retired and Coach Martinez was moved up from coaching JV to replace him. After becoming the Varsity coach, Coach Martinez's did a complete 180 when it came to basketball. Here, let me explain. Listen carefully because this is the truth I know a lot of basketball supporters in Davis would like to hear about.

I was by far one of the best basketball players in Northern California. Wait, for a second I am going to get off track. I hear the "I Will Always Love You" by Whitney Houston playing in my living room. That song is really beautiful. This is the first time that I have actually listened to the words. Wow! Anyhow, back to the topic. Everyone knew that I was the best basketball player ever known in Davis's history. This was a fact and it was no secret. With that being said, my junior year, Coach Martinez did not start me.

That alone was a total shock. Listen to this. He only played me two minutes in the second quarter. He sometimes played me the whole third quarter. In the fourth quarter I played the last three minutes. Anyone, who was ever a star sports player, would understand how, that little bit of play time could hurt a kid. Especially when you and everyone else knows that you are the best. My play time was an average of twelve minutes per game. There are a total 32 minutes in a single high school basketball game. The numbers alone do a lot of explaining. I dealt with being mistreated for the first half of the season, until one day after practice...I decided to stay behind to speak with Coach Martinez. I will never forget this conversation and how it played out. This was a major turning point in my life and I mean for the worst. "How come you're not playing me?" I asked. "What do you mean, I am playing you," he replied. I did not like his response because he knew what I was talking about. He knew I wanted to know why he was not giving me the play time that I deserved. He began to come up with stupid reasons to why he did not play me. One reason was because I sagged my pants. That was a ridiculous thing to say because every kid on the basketball team wore their pants low. That was the style when I was growing up. Anyhow, the conversation began to get a little heated. All of the excuses that Coach Martinez was making to why he did not give me the play time that I deserved, were not good enough for me. Seconds later, one of my team mates came back into the gym because he forgot his sweat shirt. He overheard our discussion and decided to engage. "D.J is the best player on this team and if you want to win....you got to play him," said Jordash. "I don't have to do anything," said Coach Martinez. "Look, if I have to sacrifice my play time in order for D.J to play, let's do that right now. D.J works hard every day," Jordash said in response. "I'm not talking about this anymore," said Coach Martinez. At this point, Coach Martinez was feeling a little stupid for the way that he has been treating me. "You care too much about what the parents think," I said. "Your dam right I care about what the parents think," Coach Martinez said. Right then and there, I understood why he was killing my dream of being the best basketball player ever. Before, I could not quite understand but now I realize that I was an easy target. Just think about this for a second. I was the only black kid on the team, beside this other kid named Texas. Texas was a great ball player by the way. He was adopted by white parents who were really involved in his life, on and off of the court. They were so nice. They supported Texas in whatever he did. They supported Texas more than they supported their own children. They were really good people and still are. Anyhow, having that kind of support helped Texas tremendously. Pretty much, Texas was less of a target. I forgive Coach Martinez for his hurtful doing. Do you want to hear something really ironic? Three years ago, I began coaching the 7th and 8th grade boy and girl's basketball teams at Holmes Junior High. That adds up to a total of four teams that I was coaching. I learned a lot from the kids. Anyhow, guess who was at my basketball decision making disposal? Could it be Coach Martinez's first and only son trying out for my team? Yes, it was! Oh boy was I excited... excited to do the right thing. Did I mistreat this kid like his father mistreated me? Hell no! I am a real man and real men understand that all children are innocent. You could not pay me any amount of money to make me treat that kid any different from the next. I believe that all children should be handed the world on a silver platter. I mean all of that. Even though Coach Martinez took my world away, I never let him take my heart. Coach Martinez's son was a horrible basketball player. He was very scrawny, pretty much the runt of the team. He wore think glasses and he wobbled funny when he walked but I can tell you one thing....that kid worked his butt of everyday at practice!! I loved that about him. Every day, he made more and more improvement. His attitude was great. Alert and ready to learn is how he came to practice every single day. He asked great question and wanted to get better. Better is exactly what he got. Coach Martinez's son quickly became my star defender. His defense was great and his feel for the game was better. Athleticism was something he was not blessed to be born with but that does not matter because that is not how I determine how much playtime a kid receives. I have a very simple direct way of coaching. Listen to your parents, get good grades, be respectful, show up to practice, work hard and be a team player…and you will play!! It is as simple as that. You can be the best basketball player in the world but if you do not bring those qualities with you that are listed above, you can kiss your playtime goodbye. Basically, "complaining parents," could never play a role in how much playtime any of my players will receive. As you can tell, I am still bothered by my Coach Martinez's decision making. I am still really confused. I am the kind of person who wants to know and understand everything. My mother-in-law always says, "You want to understand everything because you are still young. When you get to be my age, you learn to accept thing for what they are." I know, I should be over it by now, since it has been nine years but I am really stubborn. Why do a lot unqualified people end up in a position to determine someone else's future? Okay, this is how I see it. How can someone teach another to be one of the best if that someone has never been one of the best? Coach Martinez is still the coach until this day and I find it very disturbing how he remains the coach after having 9 consecutive losing seasons. When I say losing, I mean losing badly! I am so tired of seeing kids fail because of lack of love. If Coach Martinez really cared about these kids he would have already retired. Kids from his team, stop by my house all the time asking for advice. I tell them, "...just make sure you do not quit. Don't let him take your love away from the game." These kids that drop by my house, do not suffer from lack of playtime. The problem is lack of coaching ability. You have to know how to get though to kids from all different nationalities, religions and ages. You must remember I coached these kids in junior high before they played at the high school. Their time with me was coaching at its best. The way I coached compared to the way Coach Martinez's does, is night and day for the kids. They believe in me because I can back up what I say. If I tell a 5 foot 3 kid,"keep trying to dunk the ball every day and you will soon do it," that kid will continue to try because he believes in me. I dunked at that height and I still can dunk. Relating to the kids play a big role in coaching as well. The majority of the problems that the kids come to me about...I completely understand because I have already been through it. If I do not understand something, like I said before, I am willing to listen until I do understand. Pretty much, I am the perfect person to talk to if you have something on your mind that you would like to discuss. I bet by this time, you are thinking that Coach Martinez is a total jackass...right? Well, let me be the first to tell you that you are wrong. Of the court, Coach Martinez is one of the nicest people that I have ever met. I remember when I was hungry at school; he would give me snacks out of his lunch. Coach Martinez cared about what happen to us off of the court but as soon as we hit the gym...it was all about pleasing the parents. I hate Coach Martinez's coaching, but I must say that I love him as a person outside of basketball.

If you have not yet noticed that I am as real as it gets, let me be the first to tell you. If there was an award for being the realest person on the planet...I would win it. I prefer the truth even if it will hurt me. If you are wondering what my definition of being real is...it means to be honest with yourself and others, no matter what.

Anyhow, back to where I left off. The summer before my senior year in high school, Jason died, as you already know. Soon after his death I became depressed. At the time, I did not know that I was upset and confused. Now that I look back, I realize that I was a lonely kid. Being a basketball star meant nothing. I needed someone because I truly did not have anything or anyone.

The interest letters that I received from colleges such as Oregon State, UC Irvine, Eastern Washington, Hayward State and Cal ...I threw them all away. My parents had absolutely no interest in the letters that I was receiving. Honestly, they did not even know what the letters meant. My parents did not support me. Wait, I am wrong about that. In the fourth grade, my parents bought me my first pair of Adidas basketball shoes. Did they attend any of those games, NO! But they did get me the supplies that I needed to play. Those shoes meant the world to me. Picking out those pair of shoes, was pretty much the only parent child thing that I can remember us doing together. I had to make those shoes last because I knew I was not going to be getting another pair anytime soon. When our got to the point where they had holes in them, we would duck tape them back together. Anyhow, by my parents not being there for me in the way that I needed them...caused me to make some horrible decisions. At seventeen years old, my best friend dies. He was not only my best friend. He was the only thing that I had. Jason was the first person who came straight out and told me "I think you can make it to the N.B.A!! Not now you can't, but if you keep practicing." I did not know how to respond to such a nice comment, so I put my head down and said," Yea...I gotta practice hard." I said that, when I really wanted to jump for joy and say, "Really, you really think I could make the N.B.A!!!??" With Jason gone, all I had was a bunch of memories. Memories were not enough. I needed someone real in my life and I did not have it and that is why my life began to go down the drain. I was dropping into a hole without a bottom. I completely stopped playing basketball. I played in a few tournaments at the beginning of the season, during my senior year. My love for the game of basketball demolished. I stopped going to school and I did not feel like the teachers or staff at my school, could teach me anything. Learning about Henry the 7th who threw his baby into the air, slicing it in half to share with his wife...was not what I wanted to hear about. Nobody noticed my struggle. I was fighting a war within myself and at home but nobody cared. It is either, they cared and did not want to get involved or they just flat out did not give a rat's ass about me and my future? I began to smoke weed all the time and hang around people who were going through similar situations as I was. The problem with hanging out those kinds of people is that most people, who suffer from those kinds of problems, believe that the world is against them. Once you reach that point, things change. You change from the inside out. For a person like me, back then, it takes a whole lot to make me happy and just a little to make me upset. In reality, it should be the opposite.

Some people decide to fight for the better in life and other let their past predict their future. Unfortunately, the group of people that I chose to hang out with, did not see a bright future for themselves. Thos people allowed the past to haunt them. I understand that the past is something many cannot get over but this is how I deal. First I had to realize that what happens to me in my past will always be a part of me. I also had to realize that memories fade and they rarely go away. Embrace your troubled past and use your experience to help another.

Sometimes I felt like I have done too much bad to change, or turn back. My mind was in another state. Instead of working, I stole. Instead of smiling, I frowned. Instead of listening, I spoke. Instead of crying, I held my pain inside. During that time, I can honestly say...I lost myself. Just when life could get no worst, God made it all better within a blink of an eye. Beautiful appeared, with eyes the color of the waters of the Caribbean island. Her hair is the color of a piece of drift wood that was freshly washed up to sure. She looks like a princess from Rome or something. To make a long story short, I met Jessica. Jessica is now the mother of my two children. Little did I know that God would send me the most beautiful woman on the planet? Nor did I know that he would send one that would help me achieve, my lifelong dream to play in the N.B.A.

I must admit, she has taught me the power of belief. From there, my hate instantly turned into love and compassion. Jessica and I had our children at a really early age. We were the only teens with a child. Well, we were the only ones that we ever saw around.

Anyhow, even though Jessica was pregnant, she continued to go to school. Me on the other hand, I still had some demons to fight. High school was not for me and I was not going to go attend. Jessica somehow stayed motivated, graduated high school and finished her college courses. Oh, and she manages to do a fantastic job mothering. She deserves an award or something. Actually, she deserves her own world. If I could give that to her....I would, in a heartbeat. I use to think that being a mom was as easy as 1-2-3. The reason I felt that way, was because I judged a mother's duty, based on how my mother took care of me. After watching Jessica mother our two children, my 1-2-3 conclusion changed. Watching a mother love her children is priceless. It is a full time job to love, feed and teach a child like a mother does. If being a mother was a job, I believe that women would be billionaires. Think about it. They clean the house constantly. So that is considered a house keeper. They cook breakfast, lunch and dinner. That is considered an in-house chef. They watch the kids and someone who watches kids is considered a babysitter/nanny. Do you know how much Angelina Jolie pays each of her nanny's per month?????? A lot!!! Catering to the children's needs and problems is considered a counselor, so how much does Dr. Phil make per month? This is a lot of things to do throughout the day and I am sure that I am forgetting a few things. Basically, this is a man's world but it is NOTHING without a woman. I mean that from the bottom of my heart. Often, good women go unappreciated because of the select few who stop believing that their body is a holy temple. They stop believing that they are important. I think they people forget that God made Adam and Eve, not just Adam. I believe that God created woman to take care of his world until he arrives. That is a big responsibility! I think every good woman on the planet should receive praise. The problem is that every does not think the same way that I do. Anyhow, I wrote this poem for the good women in the world. To all the real good women, this poem is for you. It is called, How to Love a Woman.

HOW TO LOVE A WOMAN

Hear her speak when she is silent, because sometimes she is too tired to talk. Tell her what she is thinking before she thinks of it, because her thoughts and your heart go hand in hand. Kiss her for no reason and really mean it, because a kiss can tell it all.

HOW TO LOVE A WOMAN
Whisper funny things in her ear, because that's what best friends do. Give her 10 reason why you love her, because she can give a thousand to why she loves you. Tell her she's a Great mother, because God knows she's trying so hard.
HOW TO LOVE A WOMAN
Tell her how important she is, because sometimes she feels invisible. Tell her she's doing a great job, because everyone needs a pat on the back. Tell her how beautiful you think she is, because the only time it matter to her...is when you say it.
HOW TO LOVE A WOMAN

Watch her while she changes her clothes, because she likes it when she catches you peeking. Hold her hand, because it a reminder of why the love matters. Rub your hands through her hair, because it turns her on, and calms her all at the same time.

HOW TO LOVE A WOMAN

Give her a hug, because she deserves it. Look her in her eyes and say "I love you with all of my heart" because if you don't, she will never know.

HOW TO LOVE A WOMAN

By: David Johnson

Hopefully, you read my poem and took it to heart. Ok, I have to get back to telling you about my life.

A few years after high school, I started attending Napa Valley College. The campus was really beautiful. Pretty much every kid that attends Napa Valley College is a million airs. People at the college would go through money like water because their parents own vineyards. I learn in college. What I learned was not taught in a classroom. I watched and learned. Here is something I realized really fast. Not all wealthy people wear the latest clothing brands or flaunt how rich they are. The wealthiest person I met drove a dirty pickup truck and wore dirty clothes. Back to the subject, I played for the Men's basketball team. I was the starting point guard and I was being watched by Cal. Shortly after I finally started to get established with the whole school/basketball situation, I had no choice but to discontinue. I could not afford it. The gas prices were really high and every dollar I spent made me feel really bad because it could have been going towards my children's needs. Perusing my goals was not more important than my kids.

As time went by, my kid began to grow up faster then what I expected. I told you about how I coached at my old junior high, right? Well, let me tell you about how my journey to the N.B.A started back up. After a practice one day, a parent of one of the players that I was coaching approached me. He handed me an envelope and said, "Here coach Johnson. Thank you for all that you do for the kids." In response I said, "I can't take this" as I tried to hand the envelope back to him. Then he pushed it back towards me and said, "Please coach, this is a gift… your insulting me." When I got home that night, I tossed the envelope on the kitchen counter and got straight into the shower. When I got out of the shower, I dried myself off, put on some body lotion. I laid down on the couch and Jessica walked up with the envelope. From this moment forward or lives would change forever and never be the same again. What rest inside of this single envelope, provided us opportunity and motivation.

I did not know that a single pair of Kings Tickets would lead to my having the opportunity to try out for their team. This is how my journey to the NBA began. Jessica was very upset with me because my lack of interest in attending a pro basketball game. I expressed to her time and time again that I do not they'll and like watching other men do exactly what I could do with a basketball. Jessica could not believe what I was saying.

She thought I was crazy. Jessica knew I played basketball, but she did not know that I could play with pros. To prove me wrong, she decided to give me a chance to prove myself. Every general manager, coach, assistant coach and team owners were contacted by her."You better start getting in shape because you're going to get your chance...just wait and see." She would say every now and again.

Six months later, we received a return call from one of the best general managers ever; Geoff Petrie of the Sacramento Kings. I was invited to attend the Sacramento Kings mini-camp and based on my performance there, I would travel

with the team to Las Vegas to participate in Summer
League. On the third and final day, I was cut. Maybe I was
a horrible basketball player? Or maybe I was just not what
they were looking for? You judge...Google me. :)

Up close in real life, pro basketball players are all very big. 6
foot 4 inches tall is considered small in the NBA. I'm only 5
foot 10, so imagine how I must have felt out there. The
same rules do apply for basketball like they did back in my
younger days. The majority of big people cannot move as
quickly as small people. I used that to my advantage.

Many more opportunities happened for me after attending
the Kings mini-camp. For one, it's allowed me to have
footage of myself playing against Pros. It pretty much
allowed me to send out footage to other NBA teams, to gain
interest. Proving that I can play and keep up at the pro level
was the key. Having it on film was even better. Our local
news station picked up my story. Jessica is the cause of all
my basketball success. She put together everything. She is a
real genius. Jessica cooks, cleans and works. She
accomplishes all of her goals and then turns to help me
accomplish all of mine. What more can a man ask for? In
reality you can't actually ask for anything more but she went

far and beyond. Jessica spoke with pretty much all of the NBA greats. Including Michael Jordan's Mother, Mrs. Jordan. Larry Bird actually spoke with her on the phone. And he took time to return her phone call and let her know that he has my basketball file on his desk. It shocks me to this day, just to think about it. Larry bird is a basketball god... And sometimes I think to myself, what the hell is he doing reviewing my basketball file? It is so amazing. It does not stop here. Pat Riley told her that he was " very interested," in having me come work out at the Miami facility. Everything was arranged with the former GM Randy Pfund. Unfortunately, the day that they were going to give me a "looksy," Hurricane Ike hit. Jessica has also received direct emails from the NBA commissioner concerning my basketball statics. The New York Times picked up my story and wrote a great piece. After the Miami heat situation fell through, it seemed like my NBA dreams were put on hold. Teams began to lead me down a never ending road of...maybes. Maybe, we can get you in for a workout. Maybe, we can add you to our summer league roster. It was maybe this and maybe that for a whole year straight. All of their maybes ended up with a, "Sorry, we filled our roster," or no response at all. Soon after realizing this horrible tactic we began contacting that D-League teams. The D-League teams showed a lot of interest but by this time, I was fed up with all of the politics that comes along with pro basketball.

Although I was cut from the Kings, I am forever grateful for the opportunity to play with Kevin Martin, Spencer Hawes, Quincy Douby, Francisco Garcia, Jason Thompson and etc.

I could never forget the energy and intensity that we all played with for those three long days. If the Kings played during the season the way they did during that week, they would have one a championship that year.

I know it seems like all I'm writing about is the bad experiences that I've had with my parents, so let's talk about some issues that I had to face concerning my brother. Let me give you the recent run down on my Brother Brian. He is always in and out of jail and he does a lot of drugs. He is living in Nevada at the moment. He is addicted to gambling and he stays in and out of motels. He has had over four children and he is not involved in any of their lives. I hate to say this but he is a lowlife.

Last year he drove his pregnant teenage girlfriend Oak, from Nevada to California. Brian dropped oak off at our mother Irene's trailer in Davis. At the time, Oak was about seven months pregnant. Brian returned to Nevada alone. Oak slept on Irene's black, hot, leather couch. I know that couch was uncomfortable for her because I used to sleep on it. As time went by, I noticed Oaks stomach getting bigger and bigger. Living at Irene's house was not good for Oak or my niece that she was carrying in her belly. Irene would only allow her to eat cereal. One day, I stopped by to check how she was doing and she said, "Hungry." I asked her what she had to eat today and she said, "Two bowls of cereal."

My heart fell into my stomach. How in the world could my mom allow a pregnant woman to eat only two bowls of cereal throughout a whole entire day? I wonder if my mom forgot that her grandchild was inside of Oaks stomach? Irene's non-welcoming ways towards Oak, really upset me. Soon after that day, I made it my duty to make sure Oak, my nieces Mother had healthier food in her body to keep her baby strong.

Oak gave birth to my niece, Sky--on September 4th. I do not know if you remember but my best friend Jason died on September 4th. I guess you can call Sky's birth, "the beginning" and Jason's death, "the end." Oak gave birth to Sky in Sutter Davis Hospital. While in labor, she had no hand to hold. Oak had nothing except two random doctors to guide her through her delivery. My brother Brian was still in Nevada, scavenging the streets at night, looking for drugs. My Mom Irene did not stay in the room while Oak was giving birth because the sight of birth...she could not handle. That was weird to hear because I would assume that Irene-- mother of five children could get over such a small thing and help her daughter-in-law get through the amazing experience of giving birth. Damn, my Mom is such a confused soul. After Oak gave birth, I received a call from my Dad letting me know.

I instantly called Sutter Davis Hospital and had the operator transfer my call to her room. "Hello," Oak answered with a soft voice. "How are you feeling?" I asked. "I'm feeling okay," Oak replied. "Is the baby asleep? Is my brother happy? Did you get some cute baby clothes for her?" Yeah, she's asleep; Brian doesn't know I had the baby. I haven't talked to your brother in over three weeks. I don't have clothes for her yet," she replied. "Irene didn't get the baby any clothes?" I asked. "No, but she brought me a car seat that is way too big for a newborn baby," she said.

Hearing these horrible things upset me. It is horrible enough to have to give birth alone. Not having your child's father present at the time of your child's birth is even worst. A child is only born once. Watching your child being born should be a must. My brothers lack of must, has forced me to have hatred in my heart for him.

Oak, did not seemed excited about giving birth to her first child. Maybe it was the sound of the phone, but I really do not think so. How can I help Oak feel a little better about this situation and realize how important giving birth is? I decided to up the tone in my voice and talk about the positive things.

I told her, that she should be happy for her baby because it's hers and no matter what happens she will have something that she can love and will love her back. Jessica talked to her about baby poop and how cute it was when our kids would go potty. Basically, we were letting her know that she should be happy to have a child because there are people in the world who would die to be able to love a child of their own. Anyhow, Jessica & I decided to spend our rent money on baby supplies for Oak and Sky. We bought diapers, bottles, formula, clothes and bottle warmers, etc. We even decided to redecorate our master bedroom as a nursery and allow Oak and Sky to stay in our home until my brother got back on his feet and returned. Jessica and I slept on the living room floor. Our son and our daughter shared a room at the time. We also called around to help her get setup in an apartment so that she wouldn't have to depend on anyone.

A few days had gone by and I was receiving horrible, unthinkable, crazy message from my Mom, Irene. "Go get your own girlfriend, go have your baby and leave Brian's alone. All you want to do is use Oak so you can pay off your parking ticket," Irene screamed out on my voicemail recorder. She also said, "You are scandalous and conniving blood."

Hearing those messages confused me as well as shocked me. Irene made it seem like helping your brother's family when they are down and out was wrong. After sitting back and thinking about it for a while, I came to the conclusion that all of these things that came out of her mouth were said because that was how she felt and what she wanted to do. Oak said that Irene wanted Sky to have her last name. Oak said that freaked her out. Oak said that Irene seem like she wanted her baby. Anyhow, at this time Oak had still not heard from or seen Brian. Oak called her friend and told her to be on the look out for Brian and if she sees him, let him know that she gave birth.

A few days later Oak's friend sees Brian walking out of a McDonalds. It was late at night, so it was hard for her to see if it was him. She chased him down and told him the great news. Brian catches the bus from Nevada back to California. He knocks on my door. "Who is it?" I yell out. "Open the door man," I heard from outside. I know that voice from anywhere, I said to myself. Excited to open the door and unite him with his well taken care of family, I point towards the back of my apartment. Oak and Sky were in the nursery relaxing. Brian walks directly into the room, passing me by without saying Hi, What's up or thank you. To make it worst, he did not even have a smile on his face. I thought he would have been happy to see his baby for the first time. I guess he was not. He grabbed Sky out of Oaks arms very carelessly and said, "Lets go," in a mad tone. I did not like the way he was holding his child as if she was some type of dish towel. I turned to lock the front door because Irene was standing there instigating. I also locked the door because at the moment, I was going to beat the living shit out of Brian for being so ungrateful for my family's right doing. "Do I get a thank you?" I ask Brian. "A thank you for what," he replied. "What do you mean? A thank you for what? I made sure your kid was okay while you were gone," I said. "Whatever man," he replied.

The way my brother was acting and speaking, instantly made me realize that he was on drugs. His lips were dry and he smelled really bad. If you knew Brian like I know Brian, then you would understand. Brian would never be caught smelling or looking like that.

He left my apartment with nothing for the baby. As much as I wanted to sit there and say "whatever, it is not my problem anymore," I proceeded to bring down baby items that Brian rudely ignored...including a proper car seat. As they drove off, I continued to toss baby accessories into the car window. All this nonsense sounds pretty unrealistic, huh? Talk about swallowing your pride. At that moment, dealing with my Brother Brian's disrespect and ungratefulness...taught me that there are things in the world other than my intermediate family that I would swallow my pride for. My niece, Sky, was one of them. The whole situation hurt me more than what I expected but if I had a chance to do it all over again...I would without any hesitation. After all, it is not about my brother Brian, it is all about Sky.

My brother Darnell and I have not spoken for many moons. Not too long ago, my brother Darnell and I had an altercation that paralyzed our relationship for good. I often think about him. I wonder how he and his family are doing. The last word that I remember him saying to me is..."You're not my brother. You aren't shit to me anymore and when you see my family in the streets-- don't speak to them." I wondered where that anger came from. Actually, I do not care anymore. Well...I still care but I do not let it bother me

anymore. If anything, I should be upset with him. There
was a time when Darnell had four or five cars sitting in his
parking lot and did not offer to let me borrow one. When I
say borrow, I do not mean to just drive around and look cool.
I mean borrow one because I have two toddler children to
get from point a to point b. I worked as a campus monitor
for two hours a day that only provided $360 per month--so I
did not have enough money to buy a car for myself. The
little bit of money that I made went straight to bills. Oh and
I forgot to add...I am his brother, so asking him for help
shouldn't have even been a thought for me. Giving should
have come from him before I even realized I needed help. I
feel strongly about this because I know for a fact that is how
I would have thought. I guess the saying is true, "Just
because someone is born into your family, does not mean you
stay family." I never replied to Darnell's hurtful email. If he
could allow himself to say those kinds of things to me...then
he was right--we are not brothers. It is hard to swallow
these kinds of things because I grew up idolizing him. He
was not just my brother, he was my hero, you know? In the
morning before school, he would make sure my huge afro
was perfectly combed and shaped into a perfect circle. We
would laugh about things that only brothers could laugh
about. I remember how much he would laugh. Whenever I

saw a successful black man wearing a nice car, I would say, "He sells drugs and he wears that suit to pretend as if he doesn't." That would crack Darnell up because it was so not true. The fact that I knew absolutely nothing about the well dressed man and would say such a thing just brought tears of laughter to his eyes. As a matter of fact, I am laughing about it now. Inside jokes are something we all share and knowing that they will no longer be, hurt me. I have learned to remember all but think of the good.

As a child or should I say a toddler, I witnessed some horrible acts against a man's best friend. Although, this man's best friend was not a human being, sure did think love and protect like one. I believe this in my heart and there is nothing on the planet that can change how I feel. My first dog was a German Shepard. His name was Bosco and his coat was brown mixed with black. Bosco would always cuddle with my brothers and me. He loved us. Barking seemed to be Bosco's favorite thing to do and not because he loved to bark. Protecting us is what he lived for. The sound or feeling that he got from anything that may harm the family absolutely drove him crazy. He was more than a best friend; he was a brother to me. With that being said, it confused me to see my Dad and his friends hold poor Bosco down, open his mouth and pure hard liquor down his throat. To be exact, it was a half a bottle of E&J that they forced him to gag on. Why? Why would he do such a thing? As Bosco gagged and had to face the same burning sensation that humans endure when they take a shot of hard liquor, my heart began to ache. Bosco must have been in so much pain. The average human takes one shot and begins to clutch their chest. Bosco was forced to swallow a half of a bottle all at once. Imagine how he felt? Actually, do not imagine because allowing a horrible thought like that to enter your memory bank may cause you a lifetime of heartache. Trust me, I know. Watching my Dad and his friends laugh about it did a lot more than just satisfy their funny bone for that moment. Seeing my dog abused without anyone to teach me that those kinds of acts are wrong, caused me to put up an invisible shield. It taught me to never allow myself to become close with anything or anyone. I felt if I allowed love in my heart, then something or someone would come along and destroy it.

The list of horrible things about my past can go on forever. I am going to think of some positive memorable events in my life. Before I do so, I am going to leave you with this.

Life does not always workout the way that we planned for it to but life does guarantee one thing...experience. You can choose to use that in anyway that you would like. If you are wondering, I chose to use mine in a positive way. Most of my positive memorable events began after the birth of my son. There is nothing like having love for your own child. Soon after my son was born, along came my daughter and that produced twice the amount of love that I carry in my heart. Watching my children enjoy all of the things that I could not dream about, fulfills a great part of me. It gives me a sense of satisfaction. Seeing them happy—makes me happy. I think it is pretty cool because my kids and I share the first time experiences in pretty much everything we do. Many of their first have been my first.

Traveling to Hollywood so that I could attend the ESPY awards was done together. Stepping foot in a $14 million dollar house in the Santa Cruz Mountains was done together for the first time. The trip to Santa Cruz alone was a great experience for my children and me. No matter where you are or where you go, there will be good people around…you just have to find them. I have learned so much over the course of my life thus far. I have been blessed to learn about the history of OUR African ancestors. I have learned a lot from a person by the name of Mr. Journey. The ironic part is that I learned a lot of the truth from an old, countrified white man as well. His grandfather was a slave owner. After learning these truths about our ancestors and what the rest of the world has done and is still passively aggressively doing, I decided to write about it.

Before taking the next step to share these hidden, swept under the rug, forgotten truths…I pondered on why this old man decided to enlighten me? Why did he choose me to speak his heart to? What makes me so special to know the truths that are not written in our children's history books nor taught in all schools around the world? The world should know these truths because each country had a hand in these acts. I have concluded why I am the one that this old white man decided to teach. He knew that I would listen and learn. He knew that I would take this precious, valuable information and share it with the world like I plan to do. I feel so honored. I will give the world the truth, even if it will cost me my life. Everyone deserves the truth, even when they do not believe it. So listen people, this goes out to every race no matter what color you are. You can be black, white, purple, green, hot pink or even turquoise. The following applies to us all. This is a letter that I wrote for those of you in denial.

AFRICAN DESCENDENT

By: David L. Johnson Jr.

I was once told by an old man from Louisiana that, "White people can't handle the truth and if they did know the truth, they would do one of these two things. Place both of their hands over their ears or kill them selves because in their eyes the only truth is their truth."

Okay, let's put this old mans conclusion to the test. The majority of deaths caused by gun are caused by black people. Drugs are being distributed by black men on the majority of blocks and corners across the nation. Black people are the only race that suffers from poverty. Excuse me, suffers from poverty below what the estimated poverty level is. 80 percent of the prison population is made up of black men across America. We all agree that these things are true... right? Job well done!

It doesn't end here, that is just the beginning. The real question is this: Why are the facts above true? Could it all be because of white people or is that just a conspiracy theory that was made up? Let's take it back into time. I repeat lets take it back into time. The time is today. The past is today.

We are all living in the same day. The sun just rises and sets. Time is nothing more than a pile of numbers when it comes to determining yesterday from today.

Earlier today, you traveled on your boats to Africa, "The Mother Land." When you arrived, you saw a beautiful world filled with all different kinds of animals. You literally saw diamonds of all colors, shapes and sizes. You saw black people! You saw life at its best. Black people were cooking, singing and living. These black people did not only welcome you to their land, but they also introduced you to school.

With open arms, these black people taught you to harvest and cook, much more than just potatoes and raw meat. These black people also opened their gates for you to learn at their university. When I say university, I don't mean just any old university. I mean the first university in the world, which is located in Timbuktu, Africa.

You kneeled before their feet and learned from the same black people that you subconsciously despise today. Instead of showing our ancestors…yes our ancestor's appreciation for all that they have done for you, instead you decided to enslave them. You shot, cut and wiped the black people who loved, taught and showed compassion for you. To add insult to injury, you forced your self upon the woman of Africa.

You raped mothers and daughters. You made the innocent young black woman of Africa bear your children. It gets worse; you forced African brothers and sisters to intertwine. You literally chose the biggest, tallest and healthiest to do so.

Why?

You wanted to use their child for hard labor. Labor is what they endured. Hard physical labor! America was built from the ground up by black people. We built railroads any many other things. Bet you did not know a Black person performed the first successful open heart surgery. More of the hidden facts about African American creations and hard labor are listed below.

Biscuit Cutter	A.P. Ashbourne	Super Soaker	Lonnie Johnson
Folding Bed	L.C. Bailey	Bicycle Frame	Issac R. Johnson
Coin Changer	James A. Bauer	Space Shuttle Retrieval Arm	Wm. Harwell
Rotary	Andrew J.	Printing	W.A.

Engine	Beard	**Press**	Lavallette
Car Couple	Andrew J. Beard	**Envelope Seal**	F.W. Leslie
Letter Box	G.E. Becket	**Laser Fuels**	Lester Lee
Stainless Steel Pads	Alfred Benjamin	**Pressure Cooker**	Maurice W. Lee
Torpedo Discharger	H. Bradberry	**Window Cleaner**	A.L. Lewis
Disposable Syringe	Phil Brooks	**Pencil Sharpener**	John L. Love
Home Security System	Marie Brown	**Fire Extinguisher**	Tom J. Marshal
Corn Planter	Henry Blair	**Lock**	W.A. Martin
Cotton Planter	Henry Blair	**Shoe Lasting Machine**	Jan Matzeliger
Ironing Board	Sarah Boone	**Lubricators**	Elijah McCoy
Horse Bridle Bit	L.F.Brown	**Rocket Catapult**	Hugh MacDonald
Horse shoe	Oscar E.	**Elevator**	Alexander

	Brown		Miles
Pacemaker	Otis Boykin	**Gas Mask**	Garrett Morgan
Guide Missile	Otis Boykin	**Traffic Signal**	Garrett Morgan
Lawn Mower	John A. Burr	**Hair Brush**	Lyda Newman
Typewriter	Burridge & Marshman	**Heating Furnace**	Alice H. Paker
Train Alarm	R.A. Butler	**Airship**	J.F.Pickering
Radiation Detector	Geo. Carruthers	**Folding Chair**	Purdgy/Sadgwar
Peanut Butter	George W. Carver	**Hand Stamp**	W.B. Purvis
Paints & Satins	George W. Carver	**Fountain Pen**	W.B. Purvis
Lotion & Soaps	George W. Carver	**Dust Pan**	L.P.Ray
Automatic Fishing Reel	George Cook	**Insect Destroyer Gun**	A.C. Richardson

Ice cream Mold	A.L. Cralle	Baby Buggy	W.H. Richardson
Blood Plasma	Dr. Charles Drew	Sugar Refinement	N. Rillieux
Horse Riding Saddle	Wm. D. Davis	Clothes Dryer	G.T. Sampson
Shoe	W.A. Detiz	Celluar Phone	Henry Sampson
Player Piano	Joseph Dickinson	Pressing Comb	Walter Sammons
Arm for Recording Player	Joseph Dickinson	Curtain Rod	S.R. Scottron
Doorstop	O. Dorsey	Lawn Sprinkler	J.W. Smith
Doorknob	O. Dorsey	Automatic Gearshift	R.B. Spikes
Photo Print Wash	Clatonia J. Dorticus	Urinalysis Machine	Dewey Sanderson
Photo Embossing Machine	Clatonia J. Dorticus	Hydraulic Shock Absorber	Ralph Sanderson

Postal Letter Box	P.B. Dowing	Refrigerator	J. Standard
Toilet	T. Elkins	Mop	T.W. Stewart
Furniture Caster	David A. Fisher	Stairclimbing Wheelchair	Rufus J. Weaver
Guitar	Robert Flemming ,Jr	Helicopter	Paul E. Williams
Golf Tee	George F. Grant	Fire Escape Ladder	J.B. Winters
Motor	J. Gregory	Telephone Transmitter	Granville T. Woods
Lantern	Micheal Harney	Electric Cutoff Switch	Granville T. Woods
Thermo Hair Curlers	Soloman Harper	Relay Instrument	Granville T. Woods
Gas Burner	B.F. Jackson	Telephone System	Granville T. Woods
Kitchen Table	H.A. Jackson	Galvanic Battery	Granville T. Woods
Video	Joseph N.	Electric	Granville T.

Commander	Jackson	Railway System	Woods
Remote Controllers	Joseph N. Jackson	Roller Coaster	Granville T. Woods
Sani-Phone	Jerry Johnson	Auto Air Brake	Granville T. Woods

African American Scientists	
Benjamin Banneker (1731-1806)	Born into a family of free blacks in Maryland, Banneker learned the rudiments of reading, writing, and arithmetic from his grandmother and a Quaker schoolmaster. Later he taught himself advanced mathematics and astronomy. He is best known for publishing an almanac based on his astronomical calculations.
Rebecca Cole (1846-1922)	Born in Philadelphia, Pennsylvania, Cole was the second black woman to graduate from medical school (1867). She joined Dr. Elizabeth Benchell, the first white woman physician, in New York and taught hygiene and childcare to families in poor

	neighborhoods.
Edward Alexander Bouchet (1852-1918)	Born in New Haven, Connecticut, Bouchet was the first African American to graduate (1874) from Yale College. In 1876, upon receiving his Ph.D. in physics from Yale, he became the first African American to earn a doctorate. Bouchet spent his career teaching college chemistry and physics.
Dr. Daniel Hale Williams (1856-1931)	Williams was born in Pennsylvania and attended medical school in Chicago, where he received his M.D. in 1883. He founded the Provident Hospital in Chicago in 1891, and he performed the first successful open heart surgery in 1893.
George Washingto n Carver (1865?-1943)	Born into slavery in Missouri, Carver later earned degrees from Iowa Agricultural College. The director of agricultural research at the Tuskegee Institute from 1896 until his death, Carver developed hundreds of applications for farm products important to the economy of the South, including the peanut, sweet potato, soybean, and pecan.
Charles	A native of Cincinnati, Ohio, Turner received

Henry Turner (1867-1923)	a B.S. (1891) and M.S. (1892) from the University of Cincinnati and a Ph.D. (1907) from the University of Chicago. A noted authority on the behavior of insects, he was the first researcher to prove that insects can hear.
Ernest Everett Just (1883-1941)	Originally from Charleston, South Carolina, Just attended Dartmouth College and the University of Chicago, where he earned a Ph.D. in zoology in 1916. Just's work on cell biology took him to marine laboratories in the U.S. and Europe and led him to publish more than 50 papers.
Archibald Alexander (1888-1958)	Iowa-born Alexander attended Iowa State University and earned a civil engineering degree in 1912. While working for an engineering firm, he designed the Tidal Basin Bridge in Washington, D.C. Later he formed his own company, designing Whitehurst Freeway in Washington, D.C. and an airfield in Tuskegee, Alabama, among other projects.
Roger Arliner Young	Ms. Young was born in Virginia and attended Howard University, University of Chicago, and University of Pennsylvania, where she

(1889-1964)	earned a Ph.D. in zoology in 1940. Working with her mentor, Ernest E. Just, she published a number of important studies.
Percy L. Julian (1899-1975)	Alabama-born Julian held a bachelor's degree from DePauw University, a master's degree from Harvard University, and a Ph.D. from the University of Vienna. His most famous achievement is his synthesis of cortisone, which is used to treat arthritis and other inflammatory diseases.
Dr. Charles Richard Drew (1904-1950)	Born in Washington, D.C., Drew earned advanced degrees in medicine and surgery from McGill University in Montreal, Quebec, in 1933 and from Columbia University in 1940. He is particularly noted for his research in blood plasma and for setting up the first blood bank.
Emmett Chappelle (1925-)	Born in Phoenix, Arizona, Chappelle earned a B.S. from the University of California and an M.S. from the University of Washington. He joined NASA in 1977 as a remote sensing scientist. Among Chappelle's discoveries is a method (developed with Grace Picciolo) of

	instantly detecting bacteria in water, which led to the improved diagnoses of urinary tract infections.

African American Inventors	
Thomas L. Jennings (1791-1859)	A tailor in New York City, Jennings is credited with being the first African American to hold a U.S. patent. The patent, which was issued in 1821, was for a dry-cleaning process.
Norbert Rillieux (1806-1894)	Born the son of a French planter and a slave in New Orleans, Rillieux was educated in France. Returning to the U.S., he developed an evaporator for refining sugar, which he patented in 1846. Rillieux's evaporation technique is still used in the sugar industry and in the manufacture of soap and other products.
Benjamin Bradley (1830?-?)	A slave, Bradley was employed at a printing office and later at the Annapolis Naval Academy, where he helped set up scientific experiments. In the 1840s he developed a steam engine for a war ship. Unable to patent his work, he sold it and with the proceeds

	purchased his freedom.
Elijah McCoy (1844-1929)	The son of escaped slaves from Kentucky, McCoy was born in Canada and educated in Scotland. Settling in Detroit, Michigan, he invented a lubricator for steam engines (patented 1872) and established his own manufacturing company. During his lifetime he acquired 57 patents.
Lewis Howard Latimer (1848-1929)	Born in Chelsea, Mass., Latimer learned mechanical drawing while working for a Boston patent attorney. He later invented an electric lamp and a carbon filament for light bulbs (patented 1881, 1882). Latimer was the only African-American member of Thomas Edison's engineering laboratory.
Granville T. Woods (1856-1910)	Woods was born in Columbus, Ohio, and later settled in Cincinnati. Largely self-educated, he was awarded more than 60 patents. One of his most important inventions was a telegraph that allowed moving trains to communicate with other trains and train stations, thus improving railway efficiency and safety.
Madame	Widowed at 20, Louisiana-born Sarah

C.J. Walker (1867-1919)	Breedlove Walker supported herself and her daughter as a washerwoman. In the early 1900s she developed a hair care system and other beauty products. Her business, headquartered in Indianapolis, Indiana, amassed a fortune, and she became a generous patron of many black charities.
Garrett Augustus Morgan (1877-1963)	Born in Kentucky, Morgan invented a gas mask (patented 1914) that was used to protect soldiers from chlorine fumes during World War I. Morgan also received a patent (1923) for a traffic signal that featured automated STOP and GO signs. Morgan's invention was later replaced by traffic lights.
Frederick McKinley Jones (1892-1961)	Jones was born in Cincinnati, Ohio. An experienced mechanic, he invented a self-starting gas engine and a series of devices for movie projectors. More importantly, he invented the first automatic refrigeration system for long-haul trucks (1935). Jones was awarded more than 40 patents in the field of refrigeration.
David	Born in Nashville, Tennessee, Crosthwait

Crosthwait, Jr. (1898-1976)	earned a B.S. (1913) and M.S. (1920) from Purdue University. An expert on heating, ventilation, and air conditioning, he designed the heating system for Radio City Music Hall in New York. During his lifetime he received some 40 U.S. patents relating to HVAC systems.
Patricia Bath (1942-)	Born in Harlem, New York, Bath holds a bachelor's degree from Hunter College and an M.D. from Howard University. She is a co-founder of the American Institute for the Prevention of Blindness. Bath is best known for her invention of the Laserphaco Probe for the treatment of cataracts.
Mark Dean (1957-)	Dean was born in Jefferson City, Tennessee, and holds a bachelor's degree from the University of Tennessee, a master's degree from Florida Atlantic University, and a Ph.D. from Stanford University. He led the team of IBM scientists that developed the ISA bus—a device that enabled computer components to communicate with each other rapidly, which made personal computers fast and efficient for the first time. Dean also led the design team

responsible for creating the first one-gigahertz
computer processor chip. He was inducted into
the National Inventors Hall of Fame in 1997.

With all of that being said, you pretend to do the right thing.
You pretend as if you care. In reality, you could care less if
the black population disintegrated. Why do you feel this
way? You take every idea and accomplishment from us and
said it was yours and you did not give us credit. Instead of
hugging, you fear us. Instead of admitting we are brilliant,
you call us Niggers. Instead of admitting that Jesus has the
hair of sheep wool and the skin of bronze, you paint a picture
of him with blue eyes and call him white. Jesus is from
Africa and my hair has the same texture as sheep wool. My
skin glows in the sun like a bronze medal. Guess what race I
am? Black! The first people on earth were black!

Now that all of this is said and done, what are you doing?

I hope you are not covering you ears and I hope you do not
want to kill yourself. Instead, I hope you give black people
the same chance that we gave you.

By: David Johnson

After reading my letter, do you know what the moral of it is? If you do not know or have not thought enough about it…I will tell you. The moral is to learn the truth about what you think you know. Also, how a man can randomly walk into my life and teach truth along with changing my way of thinking for the positive.

During this small period of time, I have also learned a lot about a man by the name of John Brown, born May 9th 1800 and executed December 2nd 1859 at the age of 59. He was an abolitionist and fought for the freedom of slaves. Before I go into detail about John and his 20 children, I would like to point something out to you. The man, who spoke of pride about John Brown, is black. The Man who spoke and taught passionately of our African ancestors was white. Knowing that…taught me a lot about people. It taught me to never categorize anything or anyone. Learning things like this help me a lot in life.

John Brown was one of the few white men who fought to free slaves. John did not only fight to free slaves, he died doing so. Him and his pack of sons, gave their lives to make it possible for me to be writing this book. People like this go unheard about and I do not comprehend why!?

On the other hand we give praise to Abraham Lincoln for legally freeing slaves. The truth of the matter is....Abraham Lincoln was as racist as it gets. As a matter of fact, I bet Abraham Lincoln had slaves as well. The only reason he so-called "freed" the slaves was because the slaves were killing the captains of the ships that they were being brought over in from Africa. Taking control over the ships and overthrowing became a regular happening thing. Slaves began to cut the throats of their "Masters" while they were asleep. The slaves began to rebel and kill those who possessed slaves. Too many slave owners were beginning to come up missing and that is the real reason why Abraham Lincoln "freed" slaves.

Having the opportunity to be taught these hidden secrets of life, has been the best gift that I have ever received besides my two beautiful biracial children that God has blessed me with.

Anyhow, on to the next topic because I am starting to feel like a leader of a Black Panther organization and this is not my goal in writing this book. My goal is to explain to you how I came from absolutely nothing and became something. I became a person who learned to love and understand. Go to that from not caring at all is a huge step.

I would like to explain to you what my life has been like finding a job. This long, hard and pretty much impossible task has made me realize so much. I now understand why fathers and other black men are in prisons or have been in prison. Let's make this clear, my conclusion is not correct for all of the men that are incarcerated. This applies for many. I now understand that many of the men that are locked behind bars are nice men just like you and I. The only difference is that they realized what being black is truly about before I have. I am not saying realizing your black automatically leads you to incarceration but realizing that struggles and finding a solution is the demon. Options are slim for people like me. No one knows the struggle unless you have become one with another. When I say another, I mean with a black man. I don't mean saying, "Hi, how is your day going?" I mean loving another as if he was your brother, son, etc. Then you will truly understand what I am trying to say. I am fortunate to have come across some pretty cool white folks. As a matter of fact, I live in my 7th grade teacher's old home. He and his lovely wife decided to allow us to rent from them. I bet right now you're thinking, "Wow, big whip, your teacher allowed you to rent from him!" The part that you are missing is that he decided to trust and give us a chance when the majority of you did not.

Earlier, I spoke about giving black folks a chance, like we gave you. When I said that, I meant by doing kind acts like my 7th grade teacher. Voting for Obama does not apply. Voting for Obama does not make people any less racist, stereo-typical or close-minded. The reason I say this is because it should not have taken Obama to open your mind. It should have taken yourself. Voting for Obama was a huge step for you all, I know and understand. The true happenings start with friends, at work and school.

Make a difference yourself when it comes to issues like this. This is where I say DO NOT DEPEND ON OBAMA TO FIX THIS PROBLEM.

We all know that if he did focus on fixing this problem, people would say, "President Obama is a racist and he is choosing sides!"

My white readers, I know I have expressed a tremendous amount of concerns. It is a lot to take in for one day and people cannot change overnight, I know. Just take it a step at a time. No baby steps though!

While we are on the topic of change, let me explain what I have learned over the years about black folks.

The majority of us are too damn loud, opinionated and unreliable. When you are given a chance at a position, take it and appreciate it. Stop being late all the damn time. I know you have your own struggles, but so does everyone else. Stop bitching about where you want to be and just get there. Walk, run, skip or hitch hike. I do not give a shit about how you get there, just get there and do the best that you can. Honestly, I should take my own advice! Remember, no loud voices at work. Dress presentable and speak proper English! Slang only works in the hood, not at the work place. Black folks, you have to try to understand and fit in. White folks are not that bad, trust men. The same way you want them to understand us; they want you to understand them. If we can come to that meeting ground, everything would be fine and dandy. Before you know it, a rich white man from the suburbs will be married to a black woman from the hood name Dy-Sheeki. That would be very funny to see but in the process, I bet they could teach each other a lot. Similar to the movie starring Steve Martin and Queen Latifah. I believe the movie is called, *Bringing Down the House*. If you find sometime to relax, I advise you to rent that movie along with *Corrina Corrina, Glory,* & *Remember the Titans.*

Those movies taught me more than any school could ever teach me. Those films taught me how to love despite the differences that we all have. Love comes from a place much deeper than your heart. Love comes from the soul.

First thing's first. You have to love yourself before you love another because if you do not know what love feels like, how do you expect to provide another with it? These are the lessons learned throughout my life thus far. A black man would deny another black man before a white person would. I have learned this from past experiences. Not all black men of course. There are black men in the world that are truly "Uncle Toms." These black men that we call Uncle Toms will do everything in their will to be accepted by the white culture, even if it takes tearing down another. An Uncle Tom despises any other black man that possesses a threat. When I say threat, I do not mean, "Hey bitch, I am going to kill you on your birthday." I mean, a smart, young, black man with initiative, humor and intelligence. The only way of posing a threat to an Uncle Tom, is being more likeable to than he is by white people. I recently had to deal with one of those kinds of people. The best way to deal with an Uncle Tom is to a real and genuine person. Oh, and do not forget to smile while you're doing so. Coming in contact with these kinds of people has made me such a stronger person. I thank God for the opportunities. The funny part is that the white people that they do all of the brown nosing to, do not like them. The white folks that I know would rather interact with someone that is true to themselves and what they believe in rather than a people pleaser.

Here are a couple poems that I wrote to help black and white people understand each other a little bit better. I hope it gives a little insight.

NOT ALL OF THEM!

Not all white persons are bad!
Not all white persons hate you!
Not all white persons want to see you fail.
Not all persons use the word "Nigger."
Not all white persons believe that he/she is superior.
Not all white persons are involved with the KKK (Ku Klux
Klan)
Not all white persons have Grandparents who were slave
owners.
Not all white persons believe in slavery (John Brown)
Not all of them feel that way. How do I know? Because I
know a few.
The problem is that not all Black people understand that!!!!

By/ David Johnson

THE CYCLE CONTINUES

Caucasian man owns the companies.

Black man applies for work.

Caucasians man rejects.

Black man applies for work again and again.

Caucasians man rejects again and again.

Black man has children to feed.

Caucasian man feels that's not his problem.

Black man children stomachs are growling.

Caucasians man says "stop being lazy and go find a job!"

Black man says "what the hell… I am trying to but you keep giving the jobs to the white guys!"

Caucasians man says "stop throwing the race card."

Black man and children are now homeless.

Caucasians man is eating lobster while on a vacation in France.

Black man gut's fed up.

Caucasian man knows it.

Black man goes and robs his house and takes the items to the pond shop.

Caucasian man calls the police.

Black man exchanges item for money to buy food for his family.

Caucasians man does not understand.

Black man is happy because his family is full.

Caucasian man takes Black man to jail.

Black man faces 15 years in prison.

Caucasian man smiles with joy.

Black man children are now raised without a father.

The cycle continues.

Need I say more!??

By/ David Johnson

There is no other place on the planet like my city. This is the only place that would sit, watch and allow for something that I am about to tell you to happen. Davis is blessed to have the first pro basketball player ever in history to come from this city. Yet, they pretend as if it means nothing. You can come back home, apply for a vacant varsity head coaching position and be turned down by avoidance. How do I know this? I was the applicant. I hope you people are listening to what I am telling you? How can this be true? This is the question that you are probably asking yourself at this particular moment. I will explain. The head varsity basketball coach, Mr. Martinez is best friends with the Athletic Director, Mr. Benchell. Let me go a little further into detail. You remember Coach Martinez don't you? I spoke about him earlier. Go figure. Anyhow, this is how Benchell and Martinez works the system.

They are both Math teachers. Neither of them has played a minute of college basketball. To be completely straight forward, I believe they both grew up warming the bench.

They rotate faculty positions amongst each other so that nobody else can get hired or simply just work three or more positions at the school to keep them filled. Mr. Benchell is currently a math teacher, the athletic director, and assistant varsity boys' basketball coach with Coach Martinez. Coach Martinez is a math teacher, obviously a coach and based on how his day is going, he decides if he wants to take on the athletic director position for a while.

Here is the letter/email correspondence regarding my interest in filling the vacant coaching position:

September 11th 2008

A.D. Staff-

This is David Johnson. I reside here in Davis, Ca. (also grew up here my entire life) and I have been the 7th and 8th grade boys and girls basketball coach at Holmes Jr. High for the past 2

*years, as well as a campus monitor at Harper. I have also been
doing one-on-one basketball training with young players for a
while now. I attended Holmes Jr. High from 1995 through
1997 and then continuing on to Davis Sr. High school. During
my junior year I not only won MVP at the Vacaville tournament
but also was awarded All League by the Delta League.*

*I recently was invited personally by Geoff Petrie to attend the
Sacramento King's mini-camp. I played along side and against
Kevin Martin, Quincy Douby, Sheldon Williams, Spencer
Hawes and first-round draft pick, Jason Thompson. It was an
extraordinary opportunity that has begun to open numerous doors
for me. Believe it or not, Larry Bird, one of the All Time
Greatest, called me one day last month at about 7am in the
morning on my cell phone. The most recent; is being contacted
my Pat Riley of the Miami Heat, letting me know that he's,
"very interested." I am currently coordinating the date that I will
be flying out to Miami for a workout with GM Randy Pfund.*

*Although I am beyond thrilled about the NBA; I have always
had a special place in my heart for coaching. When I began
coaching the 8th grade boys during the '06/'07 year, they had
previously won only 2 games their entire season. That '06/'07
season, my 8th grade boys had finished 7-3. Also when I began
coaching the 8th grade girl's team last year, they had finished
their previous season with only 1 win. By the time their*

2007/2008 season was finished; we had won the Championship. When my 8th grade boys went on to play at the high school, they ended up winning only three games the entire season after having a 70% record with myself.

Being that I am 25 years old, I am confident in my ability to communicate with the kids and actually have them trust what I tell them. That is one of the top priorities that I have for coaching; to build the trust between the players and myself. When I explain something to them that they need to address, on or off the court; they don't second guess it. They know that I have done it and can still do it. They also know that I am the first basketball player from Davis that has took their basketball career this far and they know that I have the knowledge. They believe in me and I believe in them. That is how my teams succeed.

If you'd like to know my outlook on basketball, this is it: I believe that defense is the ultimate offense. If you've noticed, a majority of the players put all of their focus into offense but put absolutely no emphasis on improving their defensive skills. I appreciate someone who has the courage to go hard on BOTH sides of the floor--or at least try. I believe that anyone can throw the ball up and just by luck, it can go in. But if you have D, you can actually put a halt to all of their luck. Therefore, you never lose.

Now that I have met many important people in the basketball profession, I have contacts that can be extremely beneficial to the student athletes. I believe that once we prove ourselves with numbers then more recognition will be given to the Davis High basketball team. This will naturally result in more academic opportunities and scholarships for outstanding players.

My hopes are that you could consider me for this position as varsity girl's basketball coach. I'd like to thank you for taking the time to read my letter and for your consideration.

Proceeding this letter being sent, I received no response (please make sure you read the dates.). No reply takes this long. Why such silence? You tell me. Here is the follow-up letter that I sent:

October 27th 2008

A.D. Staff,

I have recently tried to contact the both of you regarding the varsity girls coaching position by both phone and email. I received a response, after the fact. I find that very peculiar due to the fact that my basketball resume is outstanding. I also find it really odd that the job was never posted on the DJUSD website or the EdJoin website until after the position was filled. It's ridiculous that I had to find out that JC was resigning, by random parents from the girls' varsity basketball team. Due to the publicity over the years regarding my basketball achievements here in Davis, I am appalled that neither of you took the initiative to reach out to me concerning the vacancy. There is no excuse for you lack of common courtesy. I find myself pondering the reason that both the A.D., Mr. D and asst. A.D., Mr. Benchell, are so unsupportive of my coaching endeavors.

Am I qualified? Yes, I am. More qualified than any other current or former basketball staff member in Davis. I recently was personally invited by the Sacramento Kings GM, Geoff Petrie to try out for his team. If that's not enough; I received a direct phone call from the All-Time Great, Larry Bird, to let me know he is following my story and has my information within arms length. Shall I add a few more people who showed common courtesy: Pat Riley, Don Nelson, Mitch Kupchak, Steve Kerr, Rick Sund, Chris Mullin, Mark Warkentein, Reggie Theus, Kevin Johnson, Randy Pfund, etc., etc., etc. I'm guessing that the next issue will be that I am, "over qualified." I'm beginning to get the vibe that for some apparent reason; I am unwelcome as a basketball coach at DHS. I wonder why?

I do have the ability to read between the lines. Since I am a product of Davis, I've become accustomed to the Davis philosophy from an early age. Or maybe its animosity held onto from prior years?

It just so happens that my older brother, Darnell also played basketball at DHS. He was punched in the mouth by one of Mr. Benchells' closest friends, and co-worker, Coach Martinez; who is and was the Varsity boys head basketball coach, as well as a math teacher. This is documented in the Davis Enterprise newspaper which I have. My brother was struck with such force that it caused his braces to pry apart from his teeth. Please explain or attempt to justify the reason behind this facility member's assault against a student without being reprimanded. To add insult to injury, later in the future, he was actually promoted to Athletic Director for a period of time. According to DHS's athletic dept. standards, there is a new prerequisite for coaching basketball. "You must assault at least 1 student-athlete before being considered for an open position." These are the type of things that I will not stand for or allow to be swept under the rug. I was born and raised in Davis, California and expect the same treatment that every other individual receives.

It begins with making sure our children are in proper care when involved with DHS sports and hiring coaching staff that are really qualified for the job. They should be both responsible and mentally prepared enough to deal with adolescents—in a NON physical way. Mr. D and Mr. Benchell, I hope that you will read this and in the future choose your potential coach with an unbiased point of view and with an open mind.

Look forward to hearing back from you.

Regards,

David Johnson

P.S.—I am aware of the passive aggressive response that the two of you showed proceeding my inquiry and application of the position. Unfortunately, I expected it. Also, JC is a great coach for the Varsity girls; but the method in which you came to your conclusion was truly absurd. I hope for future references, if another position at DHS opens up--- this discrimination will never again take place. Your illegal method of managing as athletic directors is questionable. I can't fathom why you are still in the position to determine coaching staff. If you haven't realized this yet, you are actually affecting people's lives in negatives ways and I will work diligently to make sure that nothing like this ever happens again.

Of course, after this proceeding email; I received a prompt reply. As a matter of fact—I received it the very same day.

What is really ironic is that even though I repeatedly state that I am interested in the HEAD VARSITY position, they respond as if I expressed interest in the "assistant chief" position. How do you result to begging the same coach that resigned, to come back so that you could avoid hiring me? Also, why would someone want to avoid hiring me as a head coach with my basketball resume? Simply Google me. Here is the reply I received:

David,

I am absolutely taken back with your e-mail and wish to meet personally with you as soon as possible.

While the initial resignation and subsequent reinstatement of Head Girls Basketball Coach happened over a period of time during which the position was advertised in the Davis Enterprise and on the EDJOIN website per usual DJUSD policy, on his reinstatement your initial inquiry was received and was forwarded on to Coach JC with our hope of your becoming involved as his head Assistant Coach.

My communication with him was that you had had a most positive interaction and were strongly considering the offer as his chief Assistant, but later decided to accept a coaching assignment from the Junior High instead.

We absolutely congratulate you on your background and recent accomplishments with the NBA, and I assure you there has never been any negative discussion regarding your desire to be part of the High School program.

In fact, we would be more than happy to have you in our program, should you reconsider.
Please let me know if you might wish for me to meet with you personally in an effort to resolve this matter, as I could come to Harper at your convenience.

Sincerely,

Mr. D

And last but not least, here is the reply that I sent:

Mr. Benchell & Mr. D,

Thank you for your prompt reply. That is a prime example of the common courtesy that I should have received from you in the beginning. When I expressed interest in the Varsity Girls Basketball Head Coaching position (not "Chief Assistant"), that was not shown. Your interest in meeting with me was what I expected when I APPLIED for the position; instead I now should have a meeting when I become a threat to exposing you & your staff? Respect is something that every person deserves. You were "taken back" by my email--- Please do not insult my intelligence. I find it rather impertinent. The going away party scheduled---CANCELLED when you became "involved." For the head coaching position which I first applied for, you may not have been against me, but I am more than certain that you weren't for it. I will not go into detail with you. In fact, I'm not interested in expressing anymore things to you that are already undeniably clear of.

Third paragraph—first and second sentence in my previous email--- completely avoided. That is another prime example of your blatant disregard. This is beginning to become offensive. By me emailing you, I thought you would come to your senses and conclude your wrong doings. Mr. D and Mr. Benchell, I am more than capable to take this to a higher authority and/or national light and will do so if need be. Obviously you're not strong believers of the saying, "the truth will set you free." Hopefully, this changes in the near future.

Best Regards,
Coach Johnson

Did they really think that by pretending that they did not receive my emails and phone call that I would let things blow over? BLOW OVER?! Allow something like this to happen? Uh....absolutely not! Basketball is my life and to have it taken away because of politics and your obvious acts of prejudice disgust me. The people that I thought were honest were deceiving. Every applicant deserves a fair shot and an interview.

My whole entire life, I have been afraid of death up until now. Wednesday, October 28th 2009 at 9:36pm. I am lying down on my couch watching an HBO series called *True Blood*. The Grandmother on this episode just passed away and they are having a funeral for her. This is one of the most important times of my life. I have always feared death. Maybe, it is because I have been close to death so many times. Bullets have barely missed me times before. Bullets have missed me a total of three times in my life. I cannot say the same for my brother. He was shot and killed about a month ago. My cousin was shot five times and luckily survived. My biological father was shot as well. So, death often crosses my mind. I have always seen death as a negative thing. Tonight, I have realized that death is another form of living. Death is just the next step to the heavens. Tonight, I visualized myself lying in a coffin. This was not just any old coffin! This was a glossy mahogany coffin. I envisioned white Christmas lights all around. Normally people have their funerals during the day time, not for me...it was at night. I pictured my funeral setting looking like the setting that the film, Twilight had at the very end of their movie. Me resting in real piece facing the beautiful stars with an open casket while everyone rejoiced with pure, unselfish, righteous, respectful and unconditional love.

Envisioning all of this made my fear of death go away. Although, I truly believe in my heart that such a perfect funeral that I explained could not happen. I did enjoy the thought though. The thought of me watching my perfect funeral was...enough I guess.

I have learned so much about life, spirituality and common sense. I have come to realize something that every woman on the planet wants to believe is untrue. I hate to break it to you but in my heart I believe that every living man cheats on his wife/girlfriend etc. If he has not cheated on you yet, it's because you are in denial, have not caught him or he just has not yet been put in the right predicament to do so. This is not something a man wants to do; it is something he was made to do. Just think about it....every male species on the planet does not stick to the same mate physically. Now, if you listened and read carefully, I said, "or he has not been put in the right predicament to do so." That means, do not, I repeat, do not allow him to be around any naked, seductive woman besides yourself or you will become another statistic. You cannot put a white man in front of a naked white woman who looks like Angelina Jolie, Jennifer Aniston, Heidi Klum or any of the women that look similar to Hugh Heffner's bunny's lol. A petite Asian girl is also a white mans kryptonite. Asian woman are known to treat their man very good. White men will resort to a loud black woman with a nice behind whenever they want to be dominated!

Black men on the other hand, pretty much will do any kind of woman. Black men are very accepting. Not because they cannot catch anything else but rather it's because they see sex as being all the same. Every race of woman has fantasized about being with a black man and we all know it! That is pretty much one of the main reasons that all other male races hate us so much. That and because we are capable of achieving anything, if we put our minds to it. Anyhow, back to the topic. A black man is a sucker for a white woman with a nice ass. Better yet-- any woman with a nice ass. Why is this? I have no idea.

Mexican men love everything under the sun as well. I have noticed that Mexican men like young women. Well....so does every other man on the planet. I think a smart, sexy, confident old woman had the advantage over all. Well, in my eyes they do.

At the moment I am rambling on an off-topic but the moral of the story is, all men cheat and if you do not want to be another statistic then I advise you to do the following:

1. Keep your eyes and thoughts on him.

2. Never talk down on him.

3. Remember how to be sexy.

4. Tell him why he is so important on a regular basis.

5. Cook for him everyday like it was your last day to cook.

6. Be spontaneous sometimes.

7. Be faithful physically, mentally, and emotionally.

Ladies--If you can honestly say from the bottom of your heart that you do those things....and your man still cheats, then I will say..."I told you so." Then I will say, "Your man is a fucking dumbass and you deserve better because if any woman can abide by those 7 terms...she is more than a woman. She is a one in a million kind of woman. Therefore you are a queen and deserve a man that can realize that and treat you like one.

So dig deep inside of yourself and pull out the truth...now answer those questions. Are you a queen?

This is only what I have come to realize and understand. You must remember...my life experiences have been a lot different from yours, so please come up with your own truth. We all have cards that we are dealt and it is your job to perceive them the way that you feel you should perceive them. In the end, only God can judge you.

As you have all realized, I am a very straight forward person. I speak from the heart. I speak only from what I know. I speak from what I feel the truth is. What I am trying to say is...find your truth and be true to them. God says it best, "Your truths shall set you free."

Anyhow, by this time you should be feeling pissed off, confused, sad, frustrated, happy or appreciative. That is my goal in writing this memoir. We all understand things in a different way and that will never change. The best part is that you are reading about my life and how I feel with an open mind. If you did not do so, you would have not been feeling any of those emotions that I stated.

I am a Davis boy from the heart. I love the ridiculous bike riders, bike paths and quiet nights. As weird as Davis may seem at some points, I must admit that it attracts some of the coolest people. Dr. James Q. Hammond, the superintended of the Davis School District has taught me more in one hour than I have learned in an entire year. He is one of those really smart guys that did not let the book smarts take over his ability to communicate with others. He talks with you, not at you or down to you. He taught me that the world does not only revolve around me. And if I want to receive, I must first give.

Oh yeah, and gay guys are some of the coolest guys that I have ever met. I was pretty close with a gay guy in high school. His name was Robear. People would make fun of him all of the time and truthfully, I would sometimes as well. I wish I could rewind time and take away all the bad things that I said about him because all he ever did was help me. He knew of a lot of my family problems. Never once did he throw my problems from home in my face. In fact, he would do the complete opposite. He would tell me how the world needs a person like me in it and how life always gets better. He would help me with the girl problems that I was having. He taught me about their likes and dislikes. He taught me, NO...he gave me reason to why I should refer to them as, "ladies" and not, "bitches." Thanks Robear...for helping me become a better person. I am so sorry if I have ever hurt your feelings.

Life is a trip sometimes. God puts people in your life and then he takes them away for one reason or another. I always seem to appreciate them most when God takes them away. I always promise myself that I will stop taking others for granted and start treasuring each and every moment that I spend with them. Does that happen accordingly? No, it does not! I am horrible at things like that. Some nights I think about it and want to cry. I have a lot to work on. If I am going to make any progress before I meet my creator, then I better start trying my best now. Tomorrow can be gone today.

When I write, I sometimes as myself, "Am I being too straight forward? Should I sugar coat some of the things that I am writing about?" That is when a little voice in the back of my mind says, "No, no, no, this is your therapy. It's about you and your life! Express yourself the best way that you know how and if they cannot accept that they are the ones who are missing out!" You can love or hate what I have to say, but please respect it.

Knowing and understanding me is a very simple thing to do. Be straight forward with me and tell me how you feel. The main cause of confrontation is not caused by what a person says, rather how it is said. Approach me with respect and I will do the same. Keep your smart allic remark to yourself unless we have established a real friendship. Even then, I might punch your lights out!!! I am joking. Ha ha, I crack myself up sometimes.

I love old people. Old people make me happy because they tell it like it is. If they hate you, them coming right out and saying it in your face is never a problem. This may sound crazy, but I respect the KKK (Klux Klan). I respect Hitler. I do not respect, agree, or even consider condoning their actions or behavior. What I do respect about them is their ability to speak the truth about what they believe in. I have never once heard about or seen Hitler or the KKK lying about their beliefs or sweeping it under the rug. I can respect an honest person, organization or group.

Like I said before, I want the truth. Lying is for cowards. If you do not like me because I am black, instead of holding a dreadful, unenthusiastic, boring conversation...please pull me to the side and say, "Look, I was raised not to associate myself with black folks, so our conversation will be pointless." You must remember...it's not what you say; it's how you say it.

I might not agree with you but, I sure would try my best to put myself in your shoes to understand where you are coming from. Knowing the root of the problem is the best way to fix it. Having someone lead you a stray is where the pain begins. Getting your hopes up for something and then having someone not hire, show up or call you back because of your race....sucks. The point that I am trying to make is...I hate sneaky, conniving people. I cannot stand them.

This situation applies for everything, not just race. It applies for gay people, white people, Indians, cat lovers, dog lovers, any and everything. I use race as my example because that's what I have been discriminated over. What I am trying to say is, "Keep it real and stop pretending."

Here is something about me that everyone always finds a bit crazy. I have never dated, kissed or held a black woman's hand in my whole entire life. I have pretty much dated only white women. It is not that I do not think black woman are attractive. I think it is because they remind me of my Mom. I often feel sad because I know that I have never allowed myself to get close to a black woman in an intimate way because of my Mom. My Mother actions during my childhood has destroyed me when it comes to this. Her lack of being a lady has made it bad for the rest. I feel bad for even saying this but it is the truth. This is the only reasoning I could come up with.

This is a poem I wrote about a very special person that I once knew. She is one of the kindest people that I have ever met.

Sweet Sadie

Our first interaction was at a birthday party that you hosted at your home, on the outskirts of Davis. Your request on my appearance was my first invitation to a party. We jumped on your trampoline and then roamed your huge home. I remember the old fashion barber chairs we sat on. Between that day and our next time of meeting, I thought of you time and time again. I thought of your open heartedness. Years later, we crossed paths ironically at the sixth grade dance. The teen center captured our moments of happiness. We danced times and time again but the last dance of the night is what I remember most. The sweet smell of perfume covered my shirt. "What kind of perfume are you wearing?" I asked as we slow danced. "I don't know...I got it from my sister. I think it's called Escape," you replied with a smile. To me, our relationship was far more than a wish. I saw you as my friend. In my heart, a friend is far more important than any crush kids like us could have. We exchanged phone numbers and I still remember the number that you gave me. From dusk until dawn we stayed awake talking on the phone. I sometimes would fall asleep, wake up and still find you there...on the line listening to me sleep. Oh, how comforting that was for me. I remember you telling me that you heard my parents fighting in the background. When I asked you what you heard, you replied with this, "Your TV. was on and so was mine so all I could hear was yelling. I was distracted from listening because I was watching one of my favorite shows. It didn't wake you so I didn't think they were being too loud." It was loud! I was just used to the fighting. The thought of your Escape perfume made me feel like I was free from it all. You made everything a lot easier. Sharing our feelings with each other though landlines phones, allowed me to escape. Thank you for everything. Thank you for your time. Thank you for your understanding. Thank you for caring for me.

By: David Johnson

Here, let me tell you a story. There once was a young man who attended college in a very economically rich city. The best of the best wines come from this beautiful place that some call The Wine Country. Personally, I call it Napa. Anyhow, while this young man was on the way to attending his first day of class at Napa Valley College...he crossed paths with a skin-head. For those of you who have no idea what a skin head is, allow me to sum it up for you. A skin-head is pretty much a group of people who only like their race. In other words, if you are Asian, Indian, Persian, Black or Brown--you should stay away from them. Normally they stick to themselves. Oh and they typically shave their heads skin bald. Back to the story, while this young man was on the way to class, he bumped shoulders with this skin-head. The young man quickly turned to the skin-head and said, "Sorry about than man." The skin-head looked at the young man with a very intense look in his eyes and then continued in his direction without saying a word. As the skin-head walked away wearing army boots with a chain dangling from his pants pocket and wearing red suspenders to keep his already high water pants up, the young man wondered why this person looked at him with such disgust. This young man was a very stubborn young man and that's why he began college in the first place. He wanted an answer to everything. Let's put it this way. If a butterfly happened to fly by him, he would wonder why and what made the butterfly choose its direction. He was far from a bad young man. In fact, he believed in holding doors for people, helping old ladies cross the street and even addresses his elders as Mr. and Mrs.

So, the young man continued on to class. When he got there, he instantly sat on the left side of the class room where it was not so crowded. A couple minutes later in came the skin-head. He sat towards the back right side of the classroom where nobody sat. The young man stood up, grabbed his backpack and headed to the area where the skin-head was sitting. "Mind if I sit over here?" The young man said. "I do," said the skin-head. "I just want to sit down-- not get married," said the young man jokingly. The skin-head found nothing comical about the young mans joke, so he ignored him.

The young man sat down in a desk, one seat behind the skin-head. Every single day, it was the same routine for both of the classmates. Every morning the young man would sit in his desk directly behind the skin-head and say, "Hey, how are you doing today? Good morning!" The same reply came from the skin-head, which was silence. The young man knew that the skin-head heard his morning hello because he would get so irritated by it, that he would start tapping his desk with his pen.

The young man figured if he is just going to sit there and listen then he might as well talk. So, after the professor finished explaining the homework for the following night, she would give students some in-class time to get ahead. That time was great for the young man because while all the other students were chatting away, he held a one man conversation with himself hoping the skin-head was listening. The young man would talk to himself as if he was in conversation with another. The skin-head was listening to every word the young man was saying. Just because a person does not respond or engage in a conversation, does not mean that person is not apart of the conversation. Anyhow, the young man would express his deepest, darkest, pain fullest secrets, while the skin-head emotionlessly soaked all of it up like a sponge. The young man took their conversations personal. He spoke of his childhood most of the time. That's where the young mans pain burns from.

One day, months later, the young man walks into the classroom and sits down in his same seat right behind the skin-head. Something was different this day. The young man did not speak to the skin-head through the 1 1/2 hours of class time. Five minutes before the class was to let out, a surprising thing happened. The skin-head spoke. He did not speak very many words but he spoke.

"You alright David?" He said unenthusiastically while staring towards the front of the classroom and sitting very sluggish in his chair. The young man responded, "Yeah-- I'm good, thanks for asking." For the next three days there was nothing but silence between the both of these classmates. On the 5th day, the skin head said, "I'm sorry about your childhood. You're a good guy, David. I don't like black people because when I was a kid I got jumped by five of them. They took my shoes and left me with bumps, scrapes and bruises." In response, the young man said, "For what it is worth...I am sorry." "So am I David," said the skin-head as he got out of his seat and placed his books into his book bag. "See ya around," the skin-head said then walked out of the classroom. By this time class was over. The weekend was here and the young man was very excited about his brief conversation with the skin-head. The young man spent his whole weekend looking forward to class on Monday. When he arrived, the seat in front of him was empty. The young man wondered where the skin-head was. The skin-head never returned, but the young man, "David," learned and took a lot with him through life from that brief conversation with the skin-head.

Take that whole story however you would like to take it, but in my eyes--it meant a lot. You come up with your own moral.

Here is one of my favorite quotes from a rapper by the name of DMX and I thought I should share it with you guys. The quote has a real strong meaning behind it once you dissect it and disregard the cursing. "Who I am is what I'll be until I die. Either accept it or don't fuck with it but if we are going to be dogs, then your stuck with it. Let me go my way but walk with me. See what I see, watch me and then talk with me. Share my pain and make it a little easier to deal with."

Do you want to know something? If I could have any job on the planet, I would be Santa Clause. Giving completes me. I often feel worthless when I have nothing to give. If I could constantly give, my life would be picture perfect. I feel lost. Seeing a smile on someone's face because of a gift or even a few kind words, helps me more than it helps the receiver. I know it sounds crazy but sometimes I would rather not exist than to sit around without helping another. I just want to give! I do not need anything in return. My gift is in the pleasure of giving. Often, people say, "I wish I was rich." Their reasoning for being wealthy is very selfish. Please do not get me wrong, everyone wants a nice warm home with a few nice cars but after that....then what? To be completely honest, none of that boils up to the feeling I get when I give. When I give to others, they say, "Thank you," but really I want to say it to them. This is something that I take very seriously.

I kind of understand why Michael Jackson gave so much. It gives a giver a feeling that I just can't explain. My feeling is probably no where near intense as the feeling that Michael Jackson felt. You know what? While we are on the topic of Michael Jackson, let me explain to all of you negative, hopping on the band wagon, no common sense having, programmed by the media, stereo typical jackasses a little about the King of Pop. Michael Jackson was not only just a singer/dancer. Michael Jackson was a healer. Through his music, he healed souls across the globe. "Heal the World," is one of many of my favorite songs that he made. When it came to giving to the poor, he gave millions and millions of dollars to people in need. America is the only place that does not realize that. All that Americans want to believe is that he is a pedophile and bleaches his skin because he is weird. Well since Michael Jackson is not here to defend himself, I am going to do it for him. If the ignorant people out there would use their own common sense, then they would realize that if Michael Jackson wanted to have sexual relations with little boys...then he could go buy thousands of little boys from some foreign country or some shit! He would not make it public that he is inviting a special selected group of children to spend a whole day with him. He opened up his home to children, allowed them to have the time of their life at one of the most beautiful amusement parks in the world, in which he had built and called, "Neverland Ranch."

The charges that were pressed against him were dropped soon after the allegations were filed. I know, I know, right now you're thinking, "Yeah, the charges were dropped because Michael Jackson paid them a ton of money to forget about it, right?" No, recently the kid, who said all of those horrible things about Michael, came out as an adult and told the world of the plot. The father of the alleged victim told the boy to lie and say that Michael touched him in a sexual way. What would a father do that for? Why would a father put his own child in harms way? Well, I will explain to you just as the now grown up alleged victim did. His father wanted money! And this would be the easiest and most convenient way to get it fast and easy.

Believe it or not, there are people in the world that do really mean things. Those kinds of people prey on the kind-hearted. They try to take the love that you have in your heart and make you believe that it is wrong. Just think about it...have you ever gave a bum on the street a dollar? Okay, that same bum will see you again the next day and make it a point to ask you for another dollar, right? That is because he realized that you have a heart for giving. When people like that realize that you have a weakness, they tend to attack it and abuse it the best way that they know how. That is exactly what those people did to Michael Jackson.

See, you people need to start thinking outside of the box and use common sense. You only live once, so start living smart. To all of you stubborn, jealous people, kiss my ass!!!

P.S.- His skin was white because he had a very bad skin problem where he lost the pigmentation. The only think that I cannot vouch for is his plastic surgery. I do not know why he got it done or when. People get plastic surgery done everyday. Some people say it becomes addictive just like getting tattoos. After you get the first one, you always want another.

Most people forget about all of the nice things that people have done for them throughout their lives. Not me! I hold those memories dear and that is why I wrote this acknowledge note.

Thank You

Jason, thank you for believing in me, like a proud father watching his disabled child achieve. Joshua, you showed me what the true definition of real is. Raymone, your desire to be rich has taught me how to strive for what you want. Just so that you know, all the nights that you and your family allowed me to sleep over...were truly needed, Dustin. Will, thank you for your expertise. I know that I can count on you, like the four seasons of Chicago. Ty, it was you and Dwight who believed that I could do anything. Your belief in me still has not altered in 20 years and I am forever grateful for that. Mrs. Foster, thank you for helping me become a better person. I still have a long way to go but I am gradually making progress. Brandon, your love has made me a strong man. I have taught me to love another because of their heart and not their skin color. Lauri, you are the Mother to every lost child and nothing can or will ever replace that. Your warm smile made everything okay for me, even when it really was not. Your son Tellas is my brother, not because of our same complexion but because he showed me how to have respect for others. Quntar, your laughter, smile and jokes kept me alive. Mrs. Chalfant, opening your home to me was like an abandoned child's soul finding heaven. Mr. K, it was you who showed me that there are other creatures on the planet who love to be loved. Mr. Roden, when I was 12 years old, you yelled and I understood. You yelled for a reason. You yelled because you wanted me to understand that you felt my pain. We both come from the same place. Mr. & Mrs. Travis, your warm embrace that I have received from you both since I was in the 7th grade has been vital. Believe it or not, that alone kept my backbone intact. Lance, your realness and encouragement made me test my limit. Without doing so, I would have not made it this far. Areola, you would talk and talk and talk. You would talk to me about sports. You would talk to me about my brother. You would talk to me, just to talk to me. Thank you, because talking to my mind off of the negative things. You bought me my first pair of basketball shoes. I remember them so vividly. Bright red Nikes with a white swoosh. You are truly the "Best Aunt" in the whole world, Tesha.

Ma, words cannot express the love that I have for you inside of my heart. Please know that you are forever my everything. Dan Gonzales, my heart was broken in two by your decision making but know that it has healed. Through our differences, you have never cheated me off of the basketball court. I remember you would always give me the snacks from your lunch to soothe my growling belly. Although it may not have seemed like much to you back then because of my ability to hide my hunger behind a smile, but trust me it did. Not because of the actual food but because you actually gave. Do you understand? I hope so. Pete Fukau, you coached me first and your love for the game still runs through my veins. Cam, you taught me what together really meant. Together, means through thick and thin. I live my life that way thanks to you. I owe you for that. I am grateful. Jean, that encouraging way of thinking is embedded in the back of my mind. Mary, teaching Jordan--taught me. Please understand that. Big Joe, you made everything okay. Your way of making something out of nothing is genius. It has been David vs. Goliath with you and I since the fourth grade and I hope that never changes. I got love for you like Bubba Sparx got love for the New South. Matt Ballin, my struggles have been your struggles since I could remember. From the trailer parks to the

Chestnut basketball courts, we are two of the same kind. Preach the word and live by it my brotha. I am sure that God is blessing you abundantly. Dave, "I expect the worst and I hope for the best," just like you taught me way back in '98. Mr. Journey, we have conquered so much together. You taught me about the truth. You showed me remedies. I told you all about the first time I grinded pepper. You listened and you did not only give me praise, you insisted that I do it again to make sure I did it right. To Ivy, I am forever a part of you. Hopefully, your way of thinking will change. My children have no Grandmother. Grandmother, they do not even know what that is. "Gooo sleep, Gooo sleep," is what you would say as you hold me in your arms to cool down my 103 degree temperature. A thing of that sort could never be lost in my memory bank, although I was just a little man at the age of three. I cannot justify your actions with...now, your past. For every action-- there is a cause and effect. Peter, you are the only father I know. You allow your weakness for my Mother to tear us apart. I now see and understand why your brothers stay far away but still near. Hopefully you come to understand. Hopefully, you want to understand. My memories of you are filled with seeing you doing kind deeds. Giving a homeless man you last dollar without a second thought, has shaped me. I am strong like a sculpture that is dried and glossed in the back of Mr. Klinger's ceramics class. Mr. Schwab, you taught me in your 7th social studies class and you are still teaching me until this day. Allowing me to watch and learn what you know has touched my heart. Opening your heart and door to my family is greatly appreciated. Repaying you for such a thing is impossible. Money, cars and diamonds are just material things, so that will not do for me to give you in return. When our time here on earth is done and we all meet the creator...I will whisper to him about the kindness that you showed my family and I. Assuming my time with him is granted. I am so far from perfect. Mrs. Corlett, your doting of me has taught me how to be a proud parent. You are the one who taught me how to write from my heart and not from my mind because the mind can forget the deepest truest thing that a heart can remember. You are the reason I passed the Hart-Bill essay. Day in and day out, you prepared us all. Just think....I am writing this book with confidence because of you. Mrs.O'Keefe, you did something for me that no other teacher would ever consider. I remember and I am touched by your understanding. You are the one and only teacher in Davis who spoke to me about black heroes who inspired you. You spoke of Martin Luther King Jr. with joy in your eyes. "Langston Hughes, was more than just a man who played saxophone. He was a poet as well," is what you explained to me. Poetry has been a big part of my life ever since, "When all aloud wind douth blow, and coughing drowns the parson's saw, and birds sit brooding in the snow, and marians bose looks red and raw," by William Shakespeare. That was taught to me by you, Mrs. Pangelene. Poetry at its best--When Daisies Pied and Violets Blued. Bob, you were there for the most important point in my basketball career. My first dunk was watched through the eyes of you; the same eyes that now watch me teach the young kids everything that I know about the game. Time has passed and you remain the same. Often people are a disappointment by remaining the same but in this case, it is remarkable. Korematsu elementary school staff, you have been great. Mrs. York, Mrs. Rinne, Mrs. Sobatka, Mrs. Arvin & Mrs. Kesser, I am so happy to see the love that you show to each student. The love that was shown for me as a child by my teachers, still exist! That is really awesome. You are helping my children become better and smarter people all around and I am forever grateful for that. Tammy, my child was feeling bad because of what another child said about his skin color. You did the magnificent. You pulled out a picture of your son and showed my son. You looked at him and said, "There is nothing wrong with your brown skin.

Your skin is beautiful. Look...my son has brown skin too."
That was really nice of you. Thanks for stepping up to the
plate. Patty, your ability to make us parents feel comfortable
is amazing. Reverend Timothy Malone, you have spoken
with me many times about my life struggles. You have
baptized my son and you have always spoken nothing but
positive words to me. "Do positive things, hang around
positive people and positive things will happen," is what you
told me very often. As time pasted, your chosen words have
come to light. Thank you. Tupac Shakur, you have taught
me more than any university could ever teach me. Your
music, poetry and your intelligence have opened my eyes to a
world that most cannot dream of seeing or understanding.
All of your music is full of guidance and enlightenment.
Your *Better Days* album was superb and needed. You make
everything a lot easier for people like us. Steve, you have
been there since the beginning so you know me better than
most. You have watched me grow from a child into a man.
I love children with all of my heart and you are the parson
that I have watched do the same. Like the saying goes,
"Watch & learn." That is what I did. Jana, thanks for all of
your support!! Robert Bell, you have my up most respect.
You have remained real and true to all things. You are a
person of fact. You are a person of common sense. People

like you in the world are not easy to find. Thanks to the
simple game of basketball, it has brought two complex,
understanding people together to talk about the truths. You,
as a white man in this day and age, have done more than
impress me. You have put your wants, desires and even
beliefs aside to find the truth! That is something most
cannot do. You have recognized the truth and struggle for
the black people of the world. You teach your class with
your heart and not your mind and that is what separates you
from the rest. You are a great mentor. In my eyes, you are
black. You are my brotha and if I ran into you on the street,
I would say, "What's up my nigga!" and shake your hand.
Although the black folks that would be hanging out with me
would look confused to why I call you, "Nigga," I would
explain to them why you are special. I would explain to
them why your skin is white but on the inside you have the
soul of an African. This is the highest form of appreciation
and gratitude that a black man can give a person, especially
when it is coming from a real person like me. Accepting you
as one of us is an honor for me. Thank You.

Before I close the last chapter of my book, I would like to
share with you my final words from my heart.

Life has brought me a long way. Through my downs, I have always risen to the challenge to overcome in a positive manner. I have a pure and noble heart and will continue to have one for the rest of my days. Having a strong heart is the key to survival. This crazy world will bring you envious people of all shapes, colors and sizes. These fakes, deceivers, liars and infiltrators will work diligently to destroy the gift that God gave us all to begin with…a righteous heart. They are too weak to be strong and that is why they hate people like you and I. Some people fail and blame themselves and some people fail and blame others. The strong believe that every setback is just a setup for a comeback. The weak believe the complete opposite. You must not let them get you down! You must not let them take away your gift. Remember to say nothing and laugh in the face of a coward. I have been to hell and back throughout my life. I often want to give up and take the easy route but there is something in the back of my mind that tells me to get up and keep moving forward. Stay on your path! If you come to an end, then create your own road and sooner or later others will follow. I have come from the ground up and the memories will forever be apart of me but I will not let them take me away from me. To the certain people who I have not spoken to, met or seen…thank you! Thank you for your support throughout my journey of life—basketball or whatever is has been; I needed it and I greatly appreciated it. It's the people behind the scenes who are the most influential. Last, but not least—thanks to all of you haters! You helped me realize what fake is and I can now simply differentiate myself from people like you.

Readers, as a gift from me to you, I would like to share with you some of my poetry that I have written over the recent years.

Sweet Heavenly Dream

Listen to my dreams. Listen to my thoughts. I dread the distance between us both. Although to me, you are now in a better place. When I dream of you…does it mean that you and I are having the exact same dream? Does it mean that we are reunited? I miss the play fighting, laughing, joking and holding deep conversation? Are we both 12 years young again or is this just a figure of my imagination? You seem alive and well. Your touch seems so real. When I close my eyes, you become reality. When I awake, you are just one of my faded memories. You are a part of my past that I will always love and treasure. Nothing can change that. You and

I both know that this world can and will beat you to your knees…if you don't get your rest. I remember looking into your eyes and hearing your silent cries. My biggest mistake is not spoken of them. This time around, I refused to leave you without words from my heart. So listen! "Your are really tired and in order for us both to move on…you most catch up on your rest………so sleep. Sleep until we dream together in the heavens above."

By/ David Johnson

Judgmental

You can ignore my heart. You can ignore my feeling. You can ignore my pain but you cannot ignore yourself. What you choose to do…is completely up to you. I will not judge you by your decisions because I have not walked in your skin. I will not judge you by your struggles because we all have our own. Nor will I judge you by your past because mine hurts. Let's make this clear, I am judging you based on the here and now. Show me who you are. Show me now, not later. Just because I am not making eye contact, does not mean I am not listening. Remember, I am judging you, based on your reasoning for not giving, when you are fully capable of doing so. Who am I to judge? I am nothing more than a poet, who believes in reading the inside of a book....and not the summery on the back cover.

If only the world could do the same.

By/ David Johnson

BEYOND READY

I am a poet. I write of my dreams. I write of my past. I write of my hopes. For now, in this moment...this is my world. These are my thoughts and I chose to share them with you. Do not take my words for granted. Hundreds of year from now, my words will mend broken hearts and heal the wounds that were left behind for scarring. The days of the counterfeits will never end but I can assure you, the days of the absolute will grow in abundance. Although you may often feel outnumbered by the heartless, perennial, permanent imposters, you must always remember...not even 1,000 humbugs can compare to a single organic mortal.

By/ David Johnson

Bewildered

Nobody understands my everyday struggle. The pain is not only mental, it is physical as well. My body hurts so badly! I wish I could show you where it hurts. I work hard every single day. Sometimes, I work so hard...the next morning it is difficult for me to stand. With time, I have no choice but to age. Each and every sun rise, I feel myself becoming a tad bit more brittle. I am not superhuman. My heart is excessively frangible, so please handle it with care. Your words, expression and actions can cause my heart to pound. I want to love you all, but I cannot give my love to everyone, at the same time. I need you but I love them. I love you but I need them. Where do I go from here? What am I saying!? I know where I should go from here but I need to................... Never mind.
Hurting people...it is wrong, no matter what the circumstances are. I'm so distracted. I need love, in every way. I need to be appreciated. I need to be understood. I need to be free. No, I need to feel free. I hope you understand?

By/ David Johnson

Alone

If you do not mind…I would like to be alone for a few
minutes? No, no…I am not upset. Disappointed, is what I
am. Please, give me a moment to myself. I carry the weight
of the world on my shoulders every single day and the load is
beginning to hurt my back. Only God knows. There is no
better healing remedy, than listening to the sound of the
ocean. The waves peacefully crashing up against the sandy
shore…completes me. This is now my better half. You have
not only lied to me but you have taken me for granted. You
have broken my heart in two and I still offered you one half.
You seem not to understand the hurt that is deep within.
You have scarred me for life. I have learned a lot from your
dishonesty and for that I will forever be grateful. Again,
please go! I would rather be alone and so should you.

By/ David Johnson

My little angel

My little angel, I am so sorry

I am sorry for not being the father that I should be. My past, my childhood and my memories have traumatized me slightly. You are far too young to understand my foregoing struggles. I am just a child raising a child. I do not know how to be the man that I need to be… for you. I am learning along the way, so take my hand and I will do my best.

My little angel, I am so sorry

I do not know how to run a business, nor do I qualify for a house loan. All I know is how to survive. I know how to subsist without the route of all evil (money.) I know how to love without the exchange for material. I know how to endure, without the without. Sounds strange, huh? I want to give you what I did not have…everything! I am learning along the way, so take my hand and I will do my best.

My little angel, I am so sorry

I am a bad father. I should be capable of giving you the sun, moon and the stars. You should be given a dollar for your every thought. I should be the one to provide every red cent. I'm supposed be your favorite superhero…but I am not. I am just another young man attempting to break the cycle. With that being said, I will continue to try…so take my hand and I will do my best.

My little angel, I am so sorry…you deserve better.

By/ David Johnson

Hidden Beauty

Unfounded beauty, lost in the depths of nowhere. Beautiful lady, love will find you. Love will track you down and fulfill your every need. Your heart is pure and do not know of a single corrupting toxic implement. You are awfully quit but yet have so much to say. Like Romanian vampire I can hear your thoughts through your eyes. In return… your eyes conclude that you are capable of doing the same. The dirt upon your clothing does not aggravate but instead ameliorate your essence. At one with nature, you walk in authentic bliss. Without a fear in the world, you look into my eyes and set me free. Your heaven is now and forever, while my heaven will only be given to me…after my last breath.

By/ David Johnson

FATHERLESS child

You dead beat heartless, sorry excuse for a father. Where have you been!? What the hell have you been doing for all these years!? Huh! Where have you been hiding!? Are you serious? Are you really my dad? Ma...hey, ma... is this the guy who left you all alone to raise five children!? Ma! Come on now ma...please tell me dis ain't him!? Dis bet not be him! Wait...let me calm down. I'm sorry if I'm yelling ma. I'm not mad at you; I'm just a little bothered at the moment. I apologize for my Ebonics but...I do not and don't want to understand people like him. I...just cannot comprehend the thought of leaving my children behind for any person, place or thing. "You have to let go and let God Dave." I can't ma...I don't know how. I don't want to know how. How come he didn't let go and let God convince him to stay and raise his children? "Stop it...if I can forgive him, then you can." You are much stronger than me though.

By/ David Johnson

Life's Changes

You are lost like a baby duckling in search of its mother. Where life may take you…you do not know. Often, you are afraid of being free the wind although you dream to be one day. Terrified of where you may end up next, you clutch enduringly on to your security blanket. With the limited amount of strength you possess, life begins to take advantage of your weakness and pierce you invariably like a thorn in the wild. Little does the atheist knows…your life, future, trials and or tribulations are not presented buy you. My advice for us all is…keeping our heads up, literally.

By/ David Johnson

Eagle-eye

As the day vanishes and the night begins to emerge, I watch and observe my surroundings. From the brittle branches that dexterously sway back and forth on the birch trees, to the lonely alley cat that walks all alone…
I watch to learn. I occasionally speak of what I see although I would rather keep my derivation to myself. Due to the fact that my truth is often misunderstood or taken for granted, I choose to verbally stay silent. My pen and pad will do just

fine. Each day I noticed something different. Who knows...
maybe tomorrow I might notice humming bird chasing a
bubble bee. I am just gleeful that I have the ability to
acknowledge.

By/ David Johnson

Coping Mechanism

My favorite time of the year is winter. Winter gives my soul
and I time to exfoliate. The strong winds seem to blow the
yearly load that I carry on my shoulders...right off. It is, as if
I can see my struggles slowly fly into the sky, then vanish
above the clouds. Similar to a red balloon filled with helium.
Just imagine a young child at a carnival, looking up into the
sky. He thinks for a moment and then he lets the string go.
Bye bye balllon....bye bye fears...bye bye.........everything.
Although, I do know... it is a lot harder than what it sounds.
The rain is a great confidant for me as well. The feeling is
unexplainable. How can I make you really understand? How
can I make you feel what I feel!? Okay...I'll try. In some
ways, the rain allows me to cry. Well...the rain cries for me.
It gives me the same feeling that crying gives you. You
know...that rejuvenated feeling...? That feeling that says
"okay, I'm over it, I needed that, I'm ready...Let's go!" That

feeling! As you all may know…I have forgotten how to cry. My past has numbed me in a bad way. But hey! If something is capable of being broken, then that something is capable of being fixed…right! We all have our own problems that we need to deal with and or overcome. In my heart, every equation becomes a problem. With every problem comes a question and with every question…you get closer to the answer. These are just a few ways that I have learned to heal myself… from myself.

By/ David Johnson

Live Learn Love

Do you think money makes you a better person? Does money boost your ego? Does it make you feel powerful…in some way? I bet it does! Not for me though. "Man makes the money, Money never makes the man." The definition of a real man/woman is not determined by the amount of money you have saved up. Being a man is based on what you decide to do with your money, after you earn it. I bet your completely satisfied going to work in the morning and then coming home to your nice, beautiful, big house…right? Let me guess, you even have a pretty white fence around your home as well? Please listen close and do not take this in the wrong way. You think you are doing your part...right!? WRONG!! Life means much more than just you and your family. See, I understand why you fear me. Wait...let me rephrase that. I comprehend why you fear me. My heart is much larger than yours and you know. You can see it by the way I walk, talk, listen and interact. Seriously, my heart knows no color. Basically, I do not care if you are Black, White, Brown, Purple, Green or even Hot Pink! My love for you cannot be altered by such a thing. Can you say the same thing for yourself and actually mean it, from the bottom of your heart?? I will not drill you too much about this because I have mercy for the weak. I even took time out to come up with the typical excuse for you. Would you like for me to quote it? No? Well, I will anyway. I think you need it. "People fear what they do not know." Feel better? Allow me to explain in detail. If there was a Black woman stranded on side of the road, with her three children...would you stop? Okay...my point proven. Now, if there was a White woman stranded on the side of the road, with her three children... would you stop? Point proven again. Just in case you are wondering, I'm not a Black panther or anything like that. I'm just a realist. If this helps you deal with the truth, my children's mother/Future Wife is Caucasian. She has the green eyes and all. Ha ha ha, I bet that tickles you. Look, you have the power to pick and choose who you would like to hire and or fire. I bet your ignorance does the majority of your firing and your insecurities do a lot of your denying.

Make a change! Be the best at what you do! Make a difference!! Give back in some way. Let's start by learning the truth…the real truth and making sure your children understand. Make this world a better place for each and every person. Learn the truth about yourself and if it is broken, then fix it. It's nothing to it but to do it.

By/ David Johnson

ORANGE PEEL

Lets all be calm. Remember to acknowledge the little things. Take the time to listen to the soft sound that an Orange makes while you are peeling it. Use your sense of smell to enjoy the clean, fresh, rejoicing scent it provides you are while doing so. That alone means a lot! Dig deeper than my words and try to understand what I am saying. An Orange is being torn apart and about to be your snack. What does the orange do in return for its abuse? It provides you with the vitamin C that your body needs to remain healthy. It gives you the sweet tangy taste that no other fruit can give. The smell is remarkable. Last but not least...it gives you...it. The Orange does not want anything in return. The Orange just wants you to be happy and to enjoy what it can offer. The fruit sounds a lot like God, right? If you ask me, I believe they share a lot of the same qualities.

This is just something to think about.

By/ *David Johnson*

You & Me Both

What are you waiting for, go apologize and make things better! Don't wait another day, life is too short! I know it's hard to say "I'm sorry" to others, when you feel like they're the ones who should be asking for your forgiveness. Why should you have to take the first step? That is what you are thinking...right? Let's get this straight...you do not have to do anything that you don't want to do. I'm just giving you my opinion. You can listen to my opinion, give a hug, be happy and be the bigger person. Options number two. You can ignore my opinion, hold a grudge and frown. Before you make your final decision, just remember...you have to work twice as many muscles in your face to frown, and then it would if you were to smile. You face is going to hurt! I can see it now, rushed into the emergency room..."my face hurts because I like to be mad. I like to frown all the time." Hey, but who am I to judge? I have a whole lot of forgiving to do myself. I also have a whole lot of apologies to make. In due time, I hope I get it these things squared away. For now, I say "tomorrow." The problem with tomorrow is that we all know that tomorrow arrives too late 98% of the time. Tomorrow for me is sometimes to short of a time period. I want to forgive but honestly...I'm not strong enough to do so. Actually, I'm just really hurt and I'm horrible at forgiving. I know I should open my heart but at this moment in time... I can't. Not because I'm not capable but because I am afraid to. My love is simple. My love is real.

Love me and I will love you back. Let me love you the best way that I know how. I love with my heart not my mind. Love or Hate is all we have in The End...make your decision.

By/ *David Johnson*

Mothers Of The Day

On this day I give thanks to all the strong, loving, supportive mothers around the world. You're the ones who keep our Earth spinning. Your gentle touch and loving words are priceless. Your inspiring actions mean more to a child then he/she can ever explain. The courage that you mothers carry on your shoulders, weighs far more than any stone a strong man can lift. The abilities that you display on a daily basis often go unnoticed. Being a hard working mother, friend and sometimes even a father figure to your child is not an easy job! Some days…I know you just want a break. Not a huge break, just a little break. A long enough break to enjoy a long hot shower, rub on lotion, and watch one of your favorite shows. Enjoying a cold glass of iced Tea and·lying under the sun, is like a stunning pair of Diamond ear rings to you at this point. As a young man at the age of 25, I want to let you know, I do understand.

Today is your day, Mother's Day…but I think your day should be everyday.

By/ *David Johnson*

Night Skies

As the sun begins to rise in Chile, above us…the fire in the sky begins to sparkle. Giving us the little bit of light that we need to manage, we become mesmerized by its glow. How can something so far away, lead us to happiness, love or children? I think about this every day. Why do the stars bring back past memories? What is it about the stars, following the lead of the moon, causes me to expose the soft spots in my heart? The power of the night skies, are even known to calm the most savage beasts. Howling, singing, roaring, talking…it all applies.

By/ *David Johnson*

WIDE EYED

I am known across America for my harsh truth. My way of expression, seem to cause others to think. Perfect! Well, think about this. "Minds are like Parachutes, they only function when open." Hear what I am saying! Why are we judged on our actions when our intentions could be good? Okay, it gets better! Here is the tricky part. What is your definition of good? Good to me could mean something horrible to you. Where does that leave us all? Let me see here...hmmm...okay, I got it! It leaves us all in a catch 22. Or should I say "stuck between a rock and a hard place?" Let's get serious here; it leaves us confused, hesitant and afraid of the new. Look, here are my words of wisdom for today. You only live once. Do not! I repeat, do not...live your life in a box.

NOW...I AM NOW SIGNING OUT. UNTIL NEXT TIME, OPEN YOUR EYES, YOUR MIND...AND YOUR HEARTS.

By/ *David Johnson*

I AM SORRY

I am sorry for your loss.
I am sorry for all your misunderstandings.
I am sorry you live in a shell.
I am sorry you are afraid of change.
I am sorry I could not be there for you.
I am sorry life is unfair.

I am sorry you have been hurt.

I am sorry that White kid called you "Nigger."

I am sorry those Black kids beat you up.

I am sorry people are selfish being.

I am sorry you can count all the honest people that you have
ever met on one hand.

I am sorry others can care less if you are in pain.

I am sorry you lost your job.

I am sorry cops feel invincible.

I am sorry White is Black.

I am sorry us as a people do not use common sense.

I am sorry you fear me.

I am sorry your father taught you wrong.

I am sorry the failure of others satisfies you.

I am sorry you are stuck in your old ways.

I am sorry for your sorrow.

I am sorry nobody has ever had sorrow for you.

I am sorry the truth hurts.

I am sorry that I am the one to have tell you.

I am sorry...I truly am.

By/ *David Johnson*

~Angel In The Dark ~

I feel like I am trapped inside of a huge cave. Every turn that
I take, seems to lead me further and further into the dark. I
can see the light but when I get within reach…it's just a
glare, a glare from the slow flowing mini streams that slide
down the side of the solid rock. It's like a lonely man walking
down a highway in search of water. In the distance, water is
present. In reality, the water you see is nothing more than a
heat wave. See….I follow all of the rules and I refuse to take
any short cuts. The part that I cannot understand is…why
have I not gained any ground? Why am I still in the same
predicament? Why am I not achieving my ultimate goals? I
am not a big fan of the whole "taste but don't swallow thing."
I've been living that way my whole life and I think it's time
for a change. How about "swallow but don't throw up?" That
is a little more reasonable for me. I can handle that. I am
ready for that! Have I not proven myself yet? Have I not
proven to you all that I am capable? I can…I have and I will
merge out of the darkness without a scratch, bump or bruise.
Without a doubt, I will stand at the top of the mountain
without a single plucked feather. Holding my head to the
sky, I become one with the breeze. The Sun becomes one
with me. I close my eyes and take a deep breath. I have

conquered everything below my feet. I am now ready to fly....Push me!

By/*David Johnson*

Listen To The Sound

Do you mind if I place my head on your chest? Would you mind if I listen to your heartbeat? I would love to listen to your story. I would love to listen to your inner song. Your heart beat has a rhythm ya know!? It is a rhythm of pounding drums, harmonicas and of a soft playing piano in the background. Shhhhh,........you have to be very quiet in order for me to hear it. I can hear when you take a deep breath. I can hear the sound of your stomach making its natural noises. I can hear the ocean! Your blood flowing sounds like a seashell .....woooooo.......woooooooo. I can hear it! Can you hear it yet? No? Well, to be completely honest, I did not expect for you to hear it. Many of people go through life without a hearing the sound because they do not allow themselves to listened to. To love another, you must give yourself. Holding back, is not an option when it comes to love. Love is a 50/50 thing. Giving a lot and taking a little is the key. If people thought in this way or even considered to think in this way, our world would be a much better place. We would all be friends, our relationships would last longer and life would not be as much of a struggle.

By/ *David Johnson*

Broken On The Floor

She cries, while he smiles.
She's being restrained, while he is the restrainer.
She is being forced, while he enforces.
She endures pain while he moans with satisfaction.
She is paper while he is scissors.
She bleeds alone, while he leaves.
She remembers, while he forgets.
She stays still, while he moves on.
She asked for help and there was none provided.

By/ *David Johnson*

Keeping You

Thing are not the same anymore. People do not help people like they should or should I say...like they know they can. I should not stereotype, but the human race sometimes confuses me. The lack of love that we show for each other is ridiculous. The lack of happiness we should have for one another when we achieve....disgust me. I truly believe that our hands are made to open up and give, not close and keep! I want everyone to win. In my eyes...there are no losers in the game of life. The only losers are the ones who forget or fail to understand that. While I'm here on this planet, YES... I will strive to make a better life for my family but at the same time I will not lose my love for others in the process. I do not know you but let's do coffee! I do not understand you but teach me more so I can learn! My beliefs are strong but I still want to know what yours are. If I can help, listen, learn, understand, compromise....I will! I will do so without regret... Will you?

By/ *David Johnson*

Fly Away

The world revolves around her, but she seems to not yet realize it. Beautiful! Very....beautiful she is, although she is not told that as often as she would like. Raising young children can be really exhausting at times. The love that she carries for her children runs deep! Like a weeping willows root that grows deep into the soil, near the swamps of Savanna Georgia. At times she feels unheard, powerless and even mistreated. She makes the best out of what she has. The mask that she wears is not of Bare Essentials. The mask is a shield that stops her from allowing her true self to shine. Afraid...it may be too much or even too little. This is every woman's thought...I'm just saying what they feel. Just for the record...be you, even if others do not understand. Live. Live, without the worry of nonsense. You only live once...please live freely. When you are free, the world gets the truth.

By: *David Johnson*

Transporter

Roll the window down and let the wind blow against your face. Stop jogging at the top of the overpasses and look down. Watch the cars past and envision yourself transporting into the passenger seat of each and every one of the drivers' vehicles. Imagine speaking with them. Allow them to express their truest, deepest thoughts to you. In return, you will do the same. After all, when your conversation is at a standstill...it will be time for you to transport into the next vehicle passing. The twist is that...if you ever cross paths with these conversation holders again, they will not remember you. You will remember every detail about them and what you spoke about. That would be sad, but it's not about you! It's about the driver and the people around you. Moral...If you take the time to get to know someone, maybe it will make you a little more considerate, understanding and caring.

Change starts with you!

By: *David Johnson*

Power Trip

Power….What a great thing to possess and/or witness being handled. In the right hands power can be a very beautiful thing. Power without envy, evil, or disrespect can be even better. It's too bad that the reasons above are pretty much a given, when you are placed in such a high position. Not for all, but for those who wear a weak muscle on their sleeve. People of power…you know who you are!!! Abusing your power is a sin. All powers are given to be used for good. That is just something to remember.

By: *David Johnson*

Ponder

She holds her busted jaw in place with her hands. On the ground crying, she looks up and mumbles, "You punk ass bitch…you broke my jaw." "I told your ass not to disrespect me," my father replied. Peeking from around the corner of the hallway…I witnessed a lifetime of future flash backs before my eyes.

Thinking to myself, "I didn't ask to be here. I didn't ask to see this." I remember my heart pounding. My heart must have skipped two beats.

"David Johnson Sr, #2577, you have visitors." Out comes my father shackled down. As he walks toward us, I notice that he has become a little bigger. He would always hit the iron whenever he was behind bars.

As he approached me and my mom, he stares me down. When he got within harms length, he would say with a straight face, "…..You better not have been fucking up…you and Spunky been fightin'?" "No…I been good," I replied with fear in my voice.

He gives me a small smile and then rubs the top of my head. My mom receives a hug from him, but not me. I guess that is…or should I say was not the manly thing to do in the 80's. Damn..hug me, I'm only 5 years old. I didn't understand that

tough guy shit at that age. It's so hard to understand. It's so
hard to forgive.

Stupid........................

By: *David Johnson*

Better Love

Stop falling in love! Stop falling love, then start treating your
lover like the ground beneath you. Love brings all together.
When brought together, please stop taking others for
granted! People seem to use love as a way to get others
attached so they can control, mistreat, and disrespect. In
reality love is supposed to do the complete opposite. Love
makes you trust, believe and respect one another. Love is not
hard. Love is only what you make of it! I try to make the best
out of mine.

By: *David Johnson*

Without A Doubt

When people become frustrated, they tend to yell. When you let your emotion get the best of you, I remain calm. I become afraid...not because of your temper or bad language. I become terrified of what extent you might attempt to go, in order to comprehend. I remain silent, until I feel you are ready. Like a Father with his son, I pat you on your back and say, "In due time." I am only 25 years old, but I am full of wisdom. I have a mindset similar to a 182 year old wizard whose beard hangs long past his chest. Stroking my imaginary beard, I ponder and think about great solutions. I want the best for my enemies, not because I care for them; but because I want their unborn children and their children's children to be happy. I am a strong believer of "...your children are a product of you." For those of you who second guess my theories....I feel sorry for you. To me, you disappear. From that day forth, you will mean no more to me than an old shelf of encyclopedia books in the back of your local library. Thinking and asking questions are always excellent! Doubting and not believing is where we end.

By: *David Johnson*

Pure Poetry

Hold your hand out in front of you, as if you're asking for
seconds. Turn on your water hose, kitchen faucet or even a
water fountain. Allow the water to fall carelessly into your
palms.

That's what I give you in my poetry. I pour my heart out.
The truth is like water...pure, refreshing and something that
we all need to survive. Survival is not making it through a
tough situation. Survival is the decisions you make after all is
said and done. Expect to be denied...Jesus was! Jesus was
denied by his closest to kin. Forgive those who do not know,
because they do not know. My poetry runs deeper than the
dark blue sea, but to you it may seem to be right above sea
level.

I forgive you.

By: *David Johnson*

Woman Kind

Her heart is the size of the empire state building. She gives without expecting anything in return. She is a sister and a daughter. In her mind, it's either you're in or you're out. She believes in no in between, later or maybe.

She holds enough love in her heart to keep a family together. Placing her feelings to the side to keep a happy home is worth the struggle of having nobody understand her. Strong! She's strong physically, mentally & spiritually.

The true definition of a woman...defines her. The beautiful Bolivian sun goddess could not compare to her beauty.

A woman devoted to honesty, loyalty and love.

By: *David Johnson*

Live for Us?!

You live for us? Are you serious? What do you mean, you live for us?! I hope that you're joking! To live for someone means...you give your love, support and tender care...no matter what. To teach your children to call you by your name and not Mom, or Mother, leaves me no choice but to question your character. My brother was dipped into boiling hot water at the age of 2. Now explain to me, how you live for us?! Explain!!......Both of his feet completely burned off! Explain!! The doctors had to cut skin from his thigh to place it onto his feet. You claim that you didn't do it...then who did?! Tell me...Who did, so I can find him and introduce myself. You live for us....yeah right!

Ok, Ok, answer this....why did I have to find out who my biological father was all on my own? Better yet, why...no, how could you lie to me for 22 years? You looked at me every day and lied to me. That hurts...

My whole life, you made me believe that the man who raised my three brothers and I was my biological father. In reality... my father is not the man who raised me, my father is his brother. To add insult to injury...you still look right into my eyes and continue to lie to me. "That test is wrong!" That is what you claim. You've had 5 different children by 5 different fathers. Again...that leaves me no choice but to question your character. That's NOT how you live for someone! You don't even know my children's middle names.

You don't live for us, you live for yourself.

Enough Said.

By: *David Johnson*

Chest Pains

Tonight I saw my brother walking down one of the busiest streets in my city. Seeing him broke my heart in two. He was all alone, alone! Damn, that's my brother...all by himself. I'm supposed to be walking right along side him, but instead...I just drove on by. Only if I could explain the hurt that I am feeling right now! Only if I could explain to you why it hurts so badly! I could give you a couple of different excuses. I was with my kids and they were tired, so I had to get them home. Or, I was not driving...so I could not stop! The truth is...I did not know how to say, "Wud up playboy; wat chu do'n?" "Do you need a ride?" Are you broke?" "Do you need a few dollars?" It has been so long since we have last spoken. The reasoning is personal. The reason combines us both. The reason is our Mother! Divide & Conquer.....

By: *David Johnson*

Crying In the Rain

He walks in the rain to hide his tears. He chooses to hide behind the water that falls from the sky, not because he is afraid...but because he loves you. He is just a young man...a young man who cries in the rain so that his tears do not sadden another. As a child, he once asked his Grandmother "Why does it rain?" In response, his Grandmother replied, "...because God is crying." So to bring himself closer to God...the young man cries when it rains. Therefore, if you see him walking in the rain, you should ask him, "Are you crying?" His response will be, "No, I'm not...we are."

By: *David Johnson*

Love, Love & Love

Throughout my life, I have watched and learned from you. The main thing that I have noticed about you is that...you are a woman of love, love and love. Throughout your ups and downs, smiles and frowns...you have always kept the love for God, others and yourself. Although, you have not once abandoned love, I know that it has abandoned you a time or two. Love hurts, comes and goes...and it can also be the best thing on earth. On this Valentine's Day, I chose you to be my Valentine because I know your love will remain and never fade. For now and forever…my love for you will do the same.

Happy Valentine's Day Grandma

By: *David Johnson*

Unspoken Words

I am you, but for some reason you treat me like a stranger. I do my best to please you but it still is not enough for you. Why must you hurt me? Your harsh words are painful. Stop hurting me! I love you, but sometimes I don't understand why? So much pressure is upon my shoulders. The world can be a heavy thing to hold…you know? Sometimes when I'm alone I begin to cry. I wish that when I cry…You would hold me in your arms and console me or even just hug me. I would never tell you these kinds of things because I am frightened by you. Please try to understand. Please try to love me. Please try not to hurt me.

By: *David Johnson*

Just Thought You'd Like To Know

I've done and achieved a lot. Throughout my life, I have accomplished things that you said I couldn't. The majority of things are held inside of my heart. I'm alive! But you would not know if that is true or not. I have two beautiful children who seem to brighten up my world a little more every day. I have one son and one daughter, David and Dajah. I even learned how to play the piano, and when I play, I think of the past.

I just thought you would like to know.

I support my family and we live in a very nice home. Oh, and yes it has wood floors. Wood flooring......who cares about wood flooring? That's not me, that's just me trying to live up to your definition of what a nice home consist of. My home has love in it, around it and under it. How's that sound for a nice home!? Did you know I work with kids everyday? I teach them that the world is theirs for the taking. I teach them the truth and they believe it. I hand others my heart everyday and I do not expect anything in return. Sometimes it's stepped on and sometimes it is even unappreciated, but

once in a while it is handled with care. I'm a man now. I
know right from wrong.

I just thought you would like to know.

I'm good with the truth and I don't know if you know that.
How is this for the truth?

Jessica, sometimes cooks like you used to. The greens, the
corn bread, and even the fried chicken! Her food tastes so
good, but what I really like about it is that.....it somehow
brings me closer to you. I have so many unanswered
questions. Why couldn't you love me? Who cares.....

These are things that I just thought you would like to know.

By: *David Johnson*

STOP

Stop holding back.
Stop hiding.
Stop putting up a shield.
Stop letting others change you.

Stop giving up.

Stop being mad and just cry.

Stop trying to please everyone.

Stop trying to be like someone else.

Stop only giving 50%.

Stop saying you can't.

Stop trying to be perfect.....

It's impossible.

By: *David Johnson*

Date of Birth

December 25th 2008, I realized. After 25 years, 6 months, and 10 days, I finally understand. Today is the day that Santa climbs down the chimney to deliver presents to the good children. Today is the day that we tell each other, "Merry Christmas." On this day we give and do not truly understand why we do so. Today we laugh, dance, eat, yell and cry. We seem to do everything except put our hands together, get on our knees, close our eyes...and say, "Happy Birthday Jesus Christ our Savior."

"Happy Birthday Father"

By: *David Johnson*

Words Can Hurt

Words from you can be so hurtful. The sound of your voice makes my heart drop into my stomach. Like a leaf falling from a half dead birch tree, I slowly break down. I weep inside, like a child who yearns for his Mother after being abandoned. I attempt to fly away, but I can't manage to succeed. I'm like a blue bird with a damaged wing, trying to hobble to safety. My breath is taken away by your limited sensitivity. Let me go! Let me live! Let me be happy.

By: *David Johnson*

Poor Boy

As you and your family gather together eating warm food and singing carols....

The poor boy stands outside all alone in the cold.

As you and your loved ones give each other hugs and kisses....

The poor boy hugs his self to keep warm.

As you take your guests' coats and hang them on a coat rack....

The poor boy begins to shiver.

As you all huddle around your beautiful fire place and laugh about your past....

The poor boy lies pressed up against the warm walls of a
factory, crying about his.
As you and your family sleep and then awake in the
morning....
The poor boy sleeps for eternity.

By: *David Johnson*

Help Me Help Myself

When the weight of the world feel like it's on your
shoulders, you must stand up. If you do not stand, nobody
else will. Why wait for help if you are not certain it will
arrive?? Sometimes the only help another needs is from
themselves. Help me! Yes, help me! Help me help myself. If
I do not learn to help myself, then I will never achieve. I do
not want you to fix my problems. I wish to repair them on
my own. If I have a flat tire, I will accept a new tire, but I
will put it on alone. Let me put it in terms of a house. I will
accept your blueprint, but I will build it myself. I want to
know how to do my part, so I do not have to wait on your
arrival.
Help Me Help Myself

By: *David Johnson*

Childhood Memories

Is there really such thing as stability? Let's see here...by the time I was a few months old, a stray bullet barely missed me. When I was 5 years old, my Mother looked right into my eyes and said, "I hate you." At age 7, I watched people be beaten up severely. As a child, I once lived in a car. To be exact, it was an old school green pinto. I'm sure that my family and I must have relocated over 20 times by the time I reached age 12. By my late teen's, my two best friends met their creator. As a child I watched my loved ones smoke crack pipes. I had no choice but to watch heroin destroy my Mothers' mind, body & soul. Tracks were left visible. Such pain was inflicted & too many bad childhood memories.

By: *David Johnson*

SILENT CRY'S

He's a man of pride. He holds his chest up high and he loves kids. He's kind-hearted and he forgives you for all of the things you did. As a kid....he said that you would beat him. Uhhm! As a kid, he said that you would barely feed him.

You tied his hands up to a pole, and you beat until he was swollen. You tore a hole through his soul and he was only nine years old. He was just a puppy. You were supposed to hold him close and say you love him. Silent screams come out, as he opens up his mouth. He's just a child. He's in pain.

How could you do this to your son, lady!!?

By: *David Johnson*

BROKEN HEARTED

You can't because I couldn't.
You won't because I wouldn't.
You're afraid because I am.
You'll drop out because I did.
You're nobody because that's what I am.
You'll cheat because I did.
You'll not cry because I couldn't.
You can't believe because I don't know how.
You can't dream because I forgot how to do so.

By: *David Johnson*

SPOKEN LIKE A TRUE KING

I love you. I love you like our savior meant for us to love each other.

Your beautiful hair blowing in the winds reminds me of a weeping willow.

A single smile from you could make the leaves on a dead tree bloom again.

My love! The thought of you not being near, makes me panic.

Your taking of a deep breath could melt the frozen ice of the North Pole. Please believe what my heart speaks.

Your presence could transform the dusty land of the Mohave Desert into a place such as Ireland in mid-spring.

Your touch could make a color blind man see pastels.

Lack of interest from you, can make a religious man contemplate suicide.

The graceful movement of bed sheets, freely hang drying on a clothesline, reminds me of your walk.

By: *David Johnson*

I ENJOY

You make me laugh. I enjoy watching you speak. I enjoy watching you think so hard. I enjoy watching you not understand me. I enjoy watching you fear me. I enjoy knowing that you think you're more intelligent than I am. I enjoy listening to your thoughts. I enjoy knowing that you truly do not like me. I enjoy knowing that I can and will defeat you if I must. I enjoy knowing why I keep you closer than my friends. I enjoy knowing why you don't. I enjoy being a nice, loving, caring person. I enjoy knowing that you hate me for it. I enjoy being real. I enjoy knowing that I know those things.

You're the joke.
You make me laugh.

By: *David Johnson*

WHO I AM TO YOU

I mean no more to you than what you allow yourself to think of me. Therefore, please take the proper and necessary steps it will take to understand me. Before you come to your conclusion, you must always gather your data. Allow me to introduce myself. "I hate to lose," although sometimes when you lose…you really win. I'll give my last to a child that is in need. I wear my heart on my sleeve. I want nothing for free. I hate to borrow, but if I have to, I'm good for it. I pay what I owe, and then some. I treat others how I want to be treated. I defend those who need defense. I'm sorry….who are you again?

By: *David Johnson*

A KISS FROM A STRANGER

It took one kiss from a stranger to change my whole life. It was so exciting! My heart was pounding, my palms were sweaty, and my stomach was turning. It felt so good. Something new, something real, something strange! In some crazy weird way, it turned me on. I knew I was not supposed to let such a thing happen, but I could not back away. Its not that I couldn't...I just did not want to. My heart already belongs to someone, but for now, it is here with this stranger. Our kiss reminded me of a warm spring day, full of love, laugher and passion. "Kiss me again" I said. "I know its wrong, but kiss me again." My body shook. My knees begin to weaken, but I wanted more. What have this stranger done to my mind, body and soul? I'll tell you what this stranger did! This stranger.........gave me what I did not know I needed, I long passionate kiss for no apparent reason. A million words could not express this kiss. I can't express this Kiss. I think you'll have to just go try it, but not with my stranger!!!

A KISS FROM A STRANGER

By: *David Johnson*

BLUE BLOODED HEART

My heart bleeds truth. My blood is blue; not Red. I look deeper, far beyond the surface. I hold my ground and stand firm in the soil; like a thousand year old oak tree. I write what I mean and mean what I write. I am no perfectionist. Although I shoot for the stars, so that if I miss...I miss! But I still land upon the moon. My every setback is just a setup for my comeback. I treasure yesterday. I enjoy today, and look forward to tomorrow. My stone cold stare may cause others to portray me as heartless Barbarian. No Barbarian here, just me focused, or lost in deep thought:) My heart skips a beat every time I look up at the beautiful Blue skies. Just the thought of the dark Blue waters pounding against the rocky shores, completes me. I am a better person now then what I was just one minute ago. I will continue to grow and make progress. My truth... is in the way I walk, so every step matters to me. My truth... is in the air, so therefore I would rather not waste my breath on nonsense. My truth...is what my heart decides for me to believe. I will continue to learn, love, and be loved for as long as my big Blue heart will allow me to. My heart is as soft as Egyptian cotton. Just for the record............my heart bleeds truth. My blood is blue; not Red.

By: *David Johnson*

HOW TO LOVE A WOMAN

Hear her speak when she is silent, because sometimes she is too tired to talk. Tell her what she is thinking before she thinks of it, because her thoughts and your heart go hand in hand. Kiss her for no reason and really mean it, because a kiss can tell it all.

HOW TO LOVE A WOMAN

Whisper funny things in her ear, because that's what best friends do. Give her 10 reason why you love her, because she can give a thousand to why she loves you. Tell her she's a Great mother, because God knows she's try so hard.

HOW TO LOVE A WOMAN

Tell her how important she is, because sometimes she feels invisible. Tell her she's doing a great job, because everyone needs a pat on the back. Tell her how beautiful you think she is, because the only time it matter to her...is when you say it.

HOW TO LOVE A WOMAN

Watch her while she changes her clothes, because she likes it when she catches you peeking. Hold her hand, because it a reminder of why the love matters. Rub your hands through her hair, because it turns her on, and calms her all at the same time.

HOW TO LOVE A WOMAN

Give her a hug, because she deserves it. Look her in her eyes and say "I love you with all of my heart" because if you don't, she will never know.

HOW TO LOVE A WOMAN

By: *David Johnson*

November 12th 2009

The day a young man defeated a pack of wild wolves and found his own way.

LaVergne, TN USA
13 July 2010
189379LV00005B/60/P